Real World 101

A Survival Guide to Life After High School

Autumn McAlpin

Sourced Media Books
San Clemente, California

For Brandon—
and impossible without the loving support of Michael.

Published by
Sourced Media Books
20 Via Cristobal, San Clemente, CA 92673 U.S.A.
www.sourcedmedia.net

ISBN: 1-4392-3983-5

Printed in the United States of America.

Contents

Introduction vi

Part 1: Surviving College 1

Chapter 1: From Applications to Acceptance: The Inside Scoop on College 3

Chapter 2: The Four-Year Plan: How to Plan Your Class Schedule So You Can Actually Graduate by Twenty-One 15

Chapter 3: Schmoozing Your Way to an "A": How to Convince Your Professor You're an "A" Student—Even If You're Not 29

Chapter 4: Writing Tips Even "-ology" Majors Need to Know 37

Chapter 5: Hitting the Books (in a Nonviolent Way) 51

Chapter 6: Justifying Socializing as Social Work: Ways to Build a Good Resume 61

Part 2: Surviving Your First Home Away from Home 71

Chapter 7: Playing House 73

Chapter 8: Windex, Pledge, and Other Strange Bottles You'll Find Under the Sink 85

Chapter 9: Get Your Security Deposit Back: How to Handle Basic Home Repairs 95

Chapter 10: How to Keep Bleeding and Shrinking Out of the Laundromat 103

Chapter 11: Getting "Customer Service, May I Help You?" to Help You 109

Chapter 12: On the Road Again. 117

Part 3: Surviving Financially 129

Chapter 13: How to Get, Keep, and Quit a Job 131

Chapter 14: From the Bank to the Balance Book: How to Set Up, Balance, and Build Your Account 143

Chapter 15: The Seven-Year Mistake: Understanding Credit 157

Chapter 16: Pay Now . . . Or Pay Later: Understanding Insurance. 167

Chapter 17: Bartering, Bargaining, and Other Ways to Annoy Salespeople 177

Chapter 18: Welcome to the World of Budgeters and Cheapskates 183

Part 4: Surviving Physically. 197

Chapter 19: Avoiding the "Freshman Fifteen" 199

Chapter 20: Pepper Spray and the Police Station: Protect Yourself! 209

Chapter 21: Call Mom, or Call 911? How to Handle Aches and Pains. 217

Chapter 22: The Difference Between Barbecuing and Boiling—and Other Cooking Basics 227

Chapter 23: Where Do They Keep the Nutmeg? And What's Nutmeg? 239

Chapter 24: Making Sure You're Not the Smelly Kid. 247

Part 5: Surviving the Social Scene 255

Chapter 25: Road Trip! 257

Chapter 26: The "It" Factor: Four Steps to Small-Town Fame 265

Chapter 27: Dating Do's and Don'ts 271

Chapter 28: It's My Party, I Can Cry if I Want to! How to Host a Party Without Too Many Tears. 281

Chapter 29: The Art of Gift-Giving 293

Chapter 30: How to Truly Live 299

Acknowledgments 307

Introduction

There's a good chance someone fed you Cheerios and dressed you in OshKosh B'Gosh during your Sesame Street years. When you went to your first sleepover, Mommy packed the bag. When you had a sniffle, Daddy took you to the doctor. What a life! The problem is—you're seventeen now, and you still don't know where they keep the luggage or how to look up the doctor's phone number!

But who needs to know how to do such things with Mom and Dad around? Guess what—as you are thrust from the commencement stage into the Real World, pampering parents are a thing of the past. You're going to have to learn a few things, and you're going to want to know them fast! How do I balance a checkbook? How do I make spaghetti? How do I get the barbecue stains out of my roommate's sweater? Aaaagh!

Don't stress—I understand. I used to be just like you. After a few years of figuring things out through trial and error (and several hundred phone calls home), I've learned the basics to surviving the chaos of the Real World, and believe me, it's much more challenging than some MTV reality show.

My eighteen-year-old brother recently moved to my town to attend a local community college. Two thousand miles away, our very worried mom asked me to help him get settled. I spent a couple of hours driving him around to sign an apartment rental agreement, get groceries, set up a bank account, and do other getting-settled-type things. Because I had already been living on my own for several years, I had forgotten how difficult doing these things can be for the first time. My brother quickly reminded me. Following are the highlights of our conversation as we sat in the car outside of the bank:

Brother: What do I do?

Me: Go in and set up an account.

Brother: What do I say?

Me: That you need to set up a checking and savings account.

Brother (blank look): How much does that cost?

Me: It should be free; banks handle your money, they don't usually charge you money. Your checks might cost a fee, but you could just get an ATM card instead.

Brother: That's the same thing as a credit card, right?

Me: No, a credit card sends you a bill and an ATM card deducts money straight out of your checking account.

Brother: How much money is in my checking account?

Me (exasperated): However much money you put in it!

Brother: But, I don't have any money.

Okay, so unfortunately most high schools don't offer a class called "Real World 101." But whether you're going to college or just moving out on your own, when you leave home for the first time, there will be many basic things you will not have a clue how to do. While doting parents mean well, their "I'll take care of it" techniques somewhat hinder their children when they enter the Real World. The Real World will not care that you never learned how to change a tire on the freeway; it will just be mad at you for blocking traffic. The bank will not care that you "forgot" to reconcile your account; they will happily charge you thirty-five bucks every time you bounce a check. Your roommates will not care that you don't know the difference between laundry detergent and fabric softener; they will just want you to stop smelling up the apartment after wearing the same socks for three weeks.

This book is meant to be a guide to handling some of the basics of grown-up life. It is written by a formerly clueless girl who encountered and endured reality—without a survival guide. And here is what I learned.

part

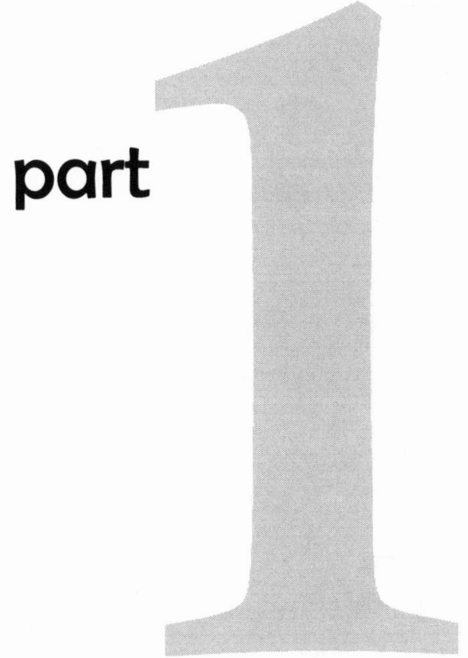

Surviving College

02:04:17

OCE-4

undefined

--execform--

Top -dict-

Top -file-
Top-1 { --disableinterrupt-- }
Top-2 --@aborted--
Top-3 { --clearinterrupt-- --disableinterrupt-- ( ) --exch-- 0 --exch-- --put-- --clear-- }
Top-4 --@aborted--

Top -dict-
Top-1 -dict-
Top-2 -dict-
Top-3 //userdict
Top-4 //globaldict

THE ADDICTION OF MARY TODD LINCOLN

ANNE E. BEIDLER

cp

coffeetownpress

Seattle, WA

For Julian,

love, Anne

The Addiction of Mrs. Lincoln was first published in 2009.

Cover design by Sabrina S. Beidler

For information regarding special discounts for bulk purchases, please contact Coffeetown Press by e-mail at:
info@coffeetownpress.com.

Library of Congress Cataloging-in-Publication Data

Beidler, Anne E., 1940-
The addiction of Mary Todd Lincoln / Anne E. Beidler.
p. cm.
Includes bibliographical references.
ISBN 978-1-60381-021-0 (alk. paper)
1. Lincoln, Mary Todd, 1818-1882--Health. 2. Lincoln, Mary Todd, 1818-1882--Mental health. 3. Presidents' spouses--United States--Biography. 4. Lincoln, Abraham, 1809-1865--Family. 5. Migraine--United States--Case studies. 6. Drug addiction--United States--Case studies. 7. Morphine abuse--United States--Case studies. I. Title.

E457.25.L55B45 2009
973.7092--dc22

2009002186

Contents

Introduction ______ *i*

A Chronology of Mary Todd Lincoln's Life ______ viii

Mary Todd Lincoln ______ ix

I: What We Know about Mary Todd Lincoln ______ *1*

Growing Up ______ 1

Wife and Mother ______ 7

Widowhood ______ 30

II: Opiate Addiction in the Nineteenth Century ______ *55*

Availability of Opiates ______ 56

Characteristics of Addicts ______ 60

Prevailing Attitudes toward Addiction ______ 67

Methods of Treatment ______ 74

Stories of Individual Addicts ______ 81

III: The Addiction of Mary Todd Lincoln ______ *95*

Did She Have a Destructive Relationship with Mood Altering Drugs? ______ 98

Was She Genetically Vulnerable to Chemical Addiction? ______ 103

What Mood-Changing Chemicals Did She Have Access To? ______ 108

In What Ways Did She Behave Like an Addict? ______ 120

What Treatment Would Have Been Available to Her? ______ 147

To Sum Up ______ 150

Appendix: What We Now Know about Chemical Addiction ______ *157*

What Is Chemical Addiction? ______ 159

Who Is Most in Danger? ______ 163

What Drugs Are Dangerous to Them? ______ 165

How Do the Victims Behave? ______ 167

What Treatment Is Available to Them? ______ 170

Bibliography ______ *173*

The evil spirit of the drug
hides its strength and touches
the doomed one gently until
it has made its grasp sure,
then claws protrude from
that soft hand and clutch
the captive with a grip which [s]he
can have little hope of breaking.

—an unnamed addict, 1881,
quoted by H. Wayne Morgan
in *Yesterday's Addicts*, 1974

Introduction

You probably know a Mary Todd Lincoln. A person in pain. A person in pain who goes to the doctor and then goes home and takes the prescribed medication whenever necessary to relieve the pain. And at first it works wonderfully. After a while, however, the dosage must be increased. And increased again. This person does not know about his or her genetic vulnerability to addiction, does not even think about addiction as relevant. All that matters is finding some measure, any measure, of relief from that pain. After all, what could possibly be wrong with relieving pain?

Yet sometimes it goes all wrong. Sometimes the pain gets destroyed but so does everything else.

The destruction began in Mary Todd Lincoln, wife of Abraham, long before she became our nation's First Lady. The destruction was slow and steady, its progress inexorable, like that of a deadly green worm eating away inside her brain. She's gone now. Her agony ended long ago, but perhaps we can learn from her suffering. Perhaps from the distance of 125 years we can look back and see a pattern that she and her family and friends could not see because it was so close and so confusing and so terrible. Mary Todd Lincoln was, after all, a wise and generous woman, and I think she would want us to know her story in the hope that some of us will not be doomed to repeat it. For there are among us still many Mary Todd Lincolns.

Let's go back. Several able tellers have told the story of the life of Mary Todd Lincoln, born into the rich and famous

Todd family, mother of four sons, wife of our Civil War President, Abraham.

Her cousin, Katherine Helm, first tried to tell the world that Mary was not nearly so difficult and peculiar and weird as the Chicago newspapers tried to make her sound. Helm told many real and touching anecdotes of their happy childhood days together. Like the time they wanted to look sophisticated and wear hoop skirts when they went to church, but had no hoops, so made their own lop-sided ones out of willow branches. It was painstaking and futile work, but they had fun.

Then Carl Sandburg, devoted to the memory of Abraham Lincoln, wanted to tell the world that anybody as wonderful as Abraham must surely have had excellent taste in a wife. Sandburg described Mary as a lovely lady and a good wife, at least at first. The fact that she became a bit crazy now and then was certainly no fault of Abraham's, according to Sandburg.

In the 1950s a respectful biographer and careful researcher, Ruth Painter Randall, wrote a meticulous story of Mary's life, the story of a loving mother, a loving wife, whose life was beset with trouble.

The Turners too, historians who gathered together Mary's existing letters, were sympathetic to Mary, who found herself in the national limelight at a tragic time. They wondered why we have built a marble temple for her husband yet still dismiss his wife as "a shrew, a spendthrift, a madwoman" (Turner 4).

More recently, the perceptive historian, Jean Baker, vividly described the tumultuous times Mary lived in and delicately suggested that Mary's troubles were psychological. Jason Emerson followed up on this explanation by describing Mary Todd Lincoln as suffering from bipolar disorder.

There is one problem, however, with each of these caring summaries of Mary Todd Lincoln's life. None of them explains the huge and awful thing that her son Robert did to his mother. Whatever made him feel he had to resort to such drastic action?

It happened in Chicago, in the year 1875, when Mary was 56 years old: [1]

> *She waited. She waited before she opened the door because she was afraid. For it seemed she lived in constant danger now, even though the war was over. Her murdered husband was already being called, "The Great One," while she, the former First Lady, the wife who had always faithfully supported him, they were calling crazy. They. If only they would leave her alone.*
>
> *That insistent knocking. Those stupid people. She tried to be always vigilant, but this time her hair was not combed, her dress was not clean. She was not expecting visitors, at least she did not think she was. But whoever was knocking, what would they think when she, looking like a common servant, opened the door herself? The old panic pushed in her throat.*
>
> *"Mrs. Lincoln," began this man, whom she had known for many years, "you are under arrest. Come with me, for they are waiting for you in court. Your insanity trial will begin in one hour."*
>
> *He seemed so business-like, almost as if he were telling her that her roof needed some minor repairs. Yet she didn't own a roof any more, and this man was not acting like an old friend, but like still another new enemy. Ever so politely, he threatened to use force, if necessary, to take her to this public trial, which her first-born son*

---

[1] Italicized passages are my attempts to imagine or reconstruct certain scenes as they might have happened.

had so carefully arranged for her. Mary Todd Lincoln went.

The President's wife, crazy? Mrs. Abraham Lincoln, arrested? And all of this arranged by her son? Yes. Her trial had been carefully planned. The judge and jury and 17 witnesses were already there waiting for her. Her son Robert was there too, of course. Her only living child, Robert Todd Lincoln, was 32, married, the father of two small children, and already a prominent and respected lawyer in Chicago.

Mary listened impassively as the witnesses recounted her erratic behavior during the recent months that she had been living in a Chicago hotel. Some of the witnesses were hotel workers, who testified that she was sometimes terrified of imaginary things, that she sometimes heard noises that no one else could hear. Other witnesses, local merchants, testified that she shopped compulsively, buying large quantities of things, like lace curtains, that she could not possibly use. Robert himself testified that although she had always been kind to him, she had been irresponsible and unpredictable since his father's murder–especially about money. For her own safety, he felt she must be restrained. And five eminent doctors testified that Mary Todd Lincoln, whom they had not recently examined, was of unsound mind.

She was insane, they all said, and legally it was so decreed. Which meant that they kept her under guard, took away control of her money, and committed her to an insane asylum. It was the nicest insane asylum they could find, but still she would be a captive there. Quite alone. She was publicly humiliated as the nation's newspapers screamed that Mrs. Abraham Lincoln was a lunatic.

This story from our national family history we perhaps do not care to remember. But it is true. Lovely, intelligent, charming Mary Todd from the rich, aristocratic and powerful Todds of Lexington, Kentucky, married that nice nobody, Abraham. They eventually had four sons, and Abraham became president and she was a good wife and a good mother and a good First Lady. Then one day she was called crazy and locked up in a lunatic asylum.

A controversy raged. Some well-meaning people thought that Mary Todd Lincoln was wrongfully incarcerated; other well-meaning people believed that at last she would receive treatment for her illness, whatever that was. At any rate, she behaved herself in the asylum for four months, and one year later, just when the newspapers had almost forgotten her, the lawyers got together again and declared her sane once more. Although legally sane, she was an ill and broken woman who wandered around Europe for a few years and then came back to her sister's home in Illinois to die.

This story of Mary Todd Lincoln's insanity trial has been well told several times before, but it seems that we have trouble remembering her story. Perhaps because her story still raises many disturbing questions. Was she really of sound mind? Why did Robert arrange such a rigged and public trial for his mother? How had such a wife as Mary, struggling with illness, affected her famous husband? And where exactly is that sometimes wobbly line between two labels, sane and insane?

Mary. Perhaps she wouldn't mind our calling her that. Mary, Mary, quite contrary. Now, she would mind that. Was she contrary? Many people have thought she was. Many historians have, straining to be charitable, pronounced her so. You see, historians seem always willing to talk about her nice husband—indeed they want to talk about that American icon—so it is hard to avoid at least a discreet mention of his perhaps contrary wife.

The historians try to be kind, really they do, but what do you say about a woman who inspired so many conflicting opinions? One of her neighbors loved her, another one hated her. One servant respected her, another one quit in disgust. One cousin described her as generous, another as stingy. One White House employee found her capable and kind, another, helpless and rude. The adjectives range in the extremes. As through the years the Lincoln name became increasingly golden, many, many people remembered Mary. Still, most of the memories are contradictory.

Remembering, after all, is a hazardous business. Imagine a journalist today trying to flesh out a person who had suddenly come under the public eye:

> *"Excuse me, sir, I'm from the newspaper, and I was just wondering what you might remember about a person you went to school with, an Elaine Wigglesworth?"*
>
> *"Who?"*
>
> *"Elaine, Elaine Wigglesworth. Many people have heard of her now, of course, but I wonder if you remember anything about her back when you were classmates in the second grade?"*
>
> *"Oh, yes. She was a good friend of mine. A lovely girl. I thought the world of Elaine."*
>
> *"So you would say, then, that there was no sign of deranged behavior back then?*
>
> *"Deranged behavior? Of course, not. She was perfectly normal, a charming girl."*
>
> *"In other words, sir, when you were second graders together you noticed nothing at all about Elaine which would indicate that she was capable of murdering a busload of school children on their way home from kindergarten?"*
>
> *"She did that?"*

> *"Thirty-seven dead, from the bomb she planted, and nine terribly injured."*
>
> *"Well, now that I think about it, Elaine Wigglesworth wasn't very well liked by the other kids. She argued constantly with the other girls. And she didn't talk to the rest of us. And once, I remember very clearly, she copied from me when we were having a spelling test. The teacher was always having to punish her. Yes, we all knew she was headed for trouble."*

And so it was, perhaps, for Mary Todd Lincoln. "Mary who? Oh, yes, I remember when. . ."

Most people being remembered, however, through the filter of collective memory, come out pretty much one way or another, good or bad. Mary Todd Lincoln's father, for example, has gone down in history as an upright, able man. Similarly, the stories that have come down to us about Abraham are positive. All the adjectives are good. The same is true of their son Robert, who lived to be much older than either of his parents. He is still usually described as intelligent, prominent, capable, responsible, private, and honest.

Then there is Mary. Mary Todd Lincoln was sometimes serene, but other times hysterical; sometimes charming and interested, but other times nasty and self-absorbed; sometimes poised, sometimes paranoid. She was, in a word, unpredictable, at least in the public part of her life. Kind historians call her an enigma.

But if we look at Mary Todd Lincoln more closely, I think we can understand her a little better. I think we need to understand her better, for, although more than a hundred years have passed between us, she was very much like many of us today. She was an addict. And as her addiction illness, which sometimes looked like craziness, worsened, the effect on her husband, who now belongs to all of us, was enormous. We must try to understand that too.

After many years of working in the field of chemical addiction, I am drawn to Mary. Any woman in our addiction therapy groups would immediately feel a kinship with her. She acts like an addict, she sounds like an addict, and she comes from a family rampant with addiction. Any recovering addict, like me, would welcome her into the room, and would feel in an instant sisterhood with her. We would understand, by sympathetic instinct, what she must have gone through, even though some of the actual hard evidence of her addiction may have disappeared from the historical record.

A Chronology of Mary Todd Lincoln's Life

Mary Todd Lincoln's life spanned from 1818 to 1882. Her 63 years included three major periods: 1) her youth, 2) her time as wife and mother, and 3) her widowhood.

Until the age of 24, Mary was the third daughter, and probably the most accomplished, of six surviving children born to Robert and Eliza Parker Todd in Lexington, Kentucky. The Todds and Parkers had been founding families in Lexington, and Mary grew up in the household of one of the richest, most prominent families in town. The Todds were the Kennedys of Kentucky.

During the second phase of her life, Mary Todd Lincoln was, in her own mind, primarily a devoted wife and mother. She married Abraham Lincoln when she was 24. Their marriage ended 23 years later when he was killed in Washington, D.C. They had four sons, two of whom died before their father did. Mary and her family spent most of this period in Springfield, Illinois, but during the last four years she was our First Lady in the White House. Throughout this time, Mary's migraine headaches plagued her. Also throughout this time, she, who was raised by slaves, remained openly opposed to slavery.

A widow at the age of 47, she spent the last 16 years of her life restlessly moving around and coping with many troubles: health, legal, and money troubles, but also relationship troubles. Spiritually, she became weary. At age 63, she died in her sister Elizabeth's home in Springfield, Illinois.

Generally speaking, Mary Todd Lincoln's biographers agree that the first phase of her life was a mostly positive time, that the last phase was a mostly negative time, and that the phase in the middle was a time full of contradictions. Let us now look at a more detailed chronology of her life. This chronology will help us see the big picture of her life and also identify the turning points where her difficulties deepened.

Mary Todd Lincoln

1818 Born in December, Lexington, Kentucky.

1825 Mary's mother died at age 31, leaving Mary's father Robert and six young children under 12: Elizabeth, Frances, Mary (age six), Levi, Ann, and infant George Rogers Clark Todd.

1826 Mary acquired a stepmother, Betsey Humphreys Todd. Betsey and Mary's father Robert then had nine more children within 15 years.

1827 At age 8 Mary went to school.

1832 Mary's sister Elizabeth married well (a bright young lawyer, son of the Illinois governor) and moved to Springfield, Illinois. Mary began attending a French school in Lexington.

1837 Mary spent some time in Springfield with her sister Elizabeth, whose house was a social center for the frontier city.

1839 At age 21, Mary moved to Elizabeth's home in Springfield and began a relationship with Abraham Lincoln, a young lawyer with neither wealth nor connections. Mary's sister and her prominent husband did not approve of this relationship. They thought Mary could do better.

1841 In January Abraham broke off his relationship with Mary.

1842 In the summer Mary and Abraham were reconciled and eventually married. They had very little money, so they lived frugally in a boarding house in Springfield. Mary learned about life without servants or slaves to care for her.

1843 Their son Robert Todd Lincoln was born. Mary Todd Lincoln was 24, and Abraham was 34.

1846 Their second son, Eddie was born. Abraham was a circuit lawyer, spending much time traveling far from home. Abraham was elected to represent Illinois in the U. S. Congress.

1847 The Lincoln family (Robert was four and Eddie, one and a half) moved to Washington, where they lived in a boarding house.

1848-49 For much of this time Mary and the boys boarded in Springfield while Abraham was in Washington, but eventually they were all settled once again in Springfield.

1850 Eddie died in February, at age four. Robert was seven. Then Willie was born in December, when Mary was 32.

1853 Tad was born.

1855 Abraham lost the race for U. S. Senate.

1856 Mary remodeled their house while her husband was away.

1858 Abraham lost Senate race again.

1859 Robert went to Harvard.

1860 Abraham elected President of United States.

1861 Lincoln family moved to Washington D.C., again, but this time not to a crowded boarding house. Mary, the new First Lady, was 42. She had her first carriage accident.

1862 Willie died.

1863 Mary had her second carriage accident.

1864 Robert graduated from college. Abraham was elected to a second term as President.

1865 Robert was appointed to Grant's staff in army. War ended. Abraham was killed in April, leaving Mary, age 46; Robert, 22; and Tad, 12.

1867 Used clothes sale.

1868 Robert married Mary Harlan. Mary and Tad went to Germany to live. *Behind the Scenes* was published by Elizabeth Keckley.

1869 Robert's first child, Mary, was born.

1871 Mary and Tad returned to U.S. and stayed at first with Robert. Tad died. Then Mary began her wandering years. The Great Fire swept Chicago.

1872 Robert's family went to Europe. Robert hired Mrs. Fitzgerald to be a nurse/companion for Mary.

1873 Robert's second child, Abraham, was born.

1875 Mary was in Florida for a while. The insanity trial was held in Chicago in May; Mary was declared insane and sent to Bellevue Sanatorium in Batavia, Illinois, where she stayed almost four months. Robert's third child, Jessie, was born in November.

1876 Mary declared legally sane in June. She left for France and another period of wandering.

1879 She fell and injured her back.

1880 She fell again on a stairway, then again on a boat. Mary came back to the U.S. She had not written to Robert while she was in Europe.

1881 Robert became Secretary of War. Robert and his daughter Mary visited Mary in Springfield for a sort of reconciliation.

1882 In July Mary died in Elizabeth's house in Springfield at age 63.

I: What We Know about Mary Todd Lincoln

Within this framework of the major events of her life, we are now ready to examine what we can be pretty sure we know about Mary Todd Lincoln as a person. Was she always an enigma? Were there signs of her "insanity" in her early years? When and in what ways did the green worm of addiction begin gnawing at her brain?

Let us look at each of the three parts of her life as carefully as we can. We will listen to her biographers, of course, but whenever possible we will listen very carefully to Mary's own words. About each of the three major periods of her life, her growing up, her wife and mother time, and her widowhood, we will try to answer four basic questions:

1. How did she look?
2. How did she feel?
3. How did she behave?
4. What things did she value most?

Growing Up

Mary spent most of this important first part of her life in Lexington, Kentucky, with her large, privileged family. She was born into luxury and prestige:

> She came into the kind of home where there was a fan-shaped window above the entrance, the gleam of silver on

> the sideboard, and rich furnishings reflected in gold-framed mirrors. There were dainty clothes, the gentle brown hands of a Negro "mammy" to receive her, and an imposing circle of relatives to exclaim over the new baby. (Randall 20)

This was the tone of the first part of Mary Todd Lincoln's life, including the years in Springfield at her sister Elizabeth's house. During these fortunate years as child, student, and socialite, Mary "had few conflicts and almost no responsibilities" (Evans 108). She seems to have been reasonably happy.

Our sources of information about her during this time include very few of her own words, for we have only three of her letters. Among her biographers, however, there is almost complete agreement about the young Mary's auspicious beginnings.

How did she look?

Mary Todd consistently appeared healthy, attractive, pretty, and well-dressed.

How did she feel?

Apparently she felt good most of the time. There is no mention of sickliness or of any physical problems that got in her way. Although she lived through a cholera epidemic as a child, she did not get the disease. Writing in 1932, W. A. Evans mentions that she had headaches since the age of 20, and Abraham implies that she had headaches sometimes when he first met her, but there is no indication that these headaches interfered with her busy life during her first 20 years. Perhaps her headaches had begun earlier, and perhaps the medicine she took for them worked better then. We cannot be sure.

How did she behave?

The people who knew Mary best saw her as intelligent, humorous, sociable, and self-confident.

Mary made no attempt to disguise her intelligence. An excellent student, she went to school much longer than most girls did. She had a good memory, a talent for acting, a love of reading, and an interest in politics. She soon became fluent in French. Mary also became a good letter writer and a good conversationalist (both highly prized accomplishments in her society). Many also found her a shrewd judge of character, "far above the average quality as regards capacity for observation, for ability to read and in other ways acquire information, and for analysis" (Evans 301).

Mary had a good sense of humor, and her early letters show her ability to laugh at herself as well as others. Her cousin told a story of Mary's about Old Sol, a down-and-out, alcoholic white man who had been sold to a black woman:

> "Oh, Elizabeth, I am so ashamed of myself! Just to think, two years ago I was laughing at him, laughing at his funny old clothes, laughing because he, a white man, had been publicly sold as a vagabond to an old negro woman for thirty cents. Oh, I was an unspeakable little beast," wept Mary. "I cannot forgive myself, but"—smiling at me through her tears—"it was a lucky bargain for the old darkey." (Helm 51)

People described young Mary as sociable, charming, lively, and interested in the activities of people around her. She was also an excellent dancer. And it was good that she excelled at these social skills, for as a young, unmarried woman, she was expected to find a husband. Indeed, she had many suitors, but, for her time, she did not marry until relatively late.

One of the reasons she was discriminating in her choice of husband was that she was apparently very self-confident. As a child she was often a leader, and as a young woman of 21 she was brave to start a new life in frontier Springfield. There a handsome, talented young lawyer, the grandson of Patrick Henry, courted her, but she wrote to her friend about him:

> "I love him not, & my hand will never be given, when my heart is not." (Turner 18)

Mary acted as if she knew her own mind and was quite comfortable with it. When she did finally marry, she pleased herself, but not her family. She was the only one of the Todd daughters to

> show some daring in her choice of husband. In the teeth of family opposition, she married Abraham Lincoln, a penniless young lawyer born in the backwoods and largely self-taught, in whom she, almost alone at first, saw greatness. (Turner 4)

Mary had full confidence in her choice.

What things did she value most?

It would seem that Mary valued her appearance and the traditional woman's role of wife and mother. In the people she loved and admired, however, it seems that she valued substance more than appearance, placing particular value on intellect, culture, and friendship.

As a child Mary told her cousin Elizabeth that when she grew up she would be perfectly satisfied with herself if she could be just like her Grandmother Humphreys (her stepmother's mother). According to her cousin, Mary meant that their grandmother was "exquisite in dress and mind and manner, the quintessence of all the elegance, virtue, and culture which Mary hoped to emulate" (Helm 34).

Throughout this first period of her life, Mary did enjoy being well-dressed. No doubt she worked hard to be exquisite in dress and manner, for such elegance would have also helped her attract a husband, a necessary part of becoming a wife and mother.

To be exquisite in mind, however, was perhaps a less universal goal for a society woman in early nineteenth-century America. Mary valued intellect in herself and in others. She read in both English and French, she kept up with politics, and she loved discussing her political views:

> By the age of fourteen she was a fiery little Whig, who could not think of enough dreadful things to say about Andrew Jackson. (Turner 7)

Another political issue on which she had a strong opinion was slavery. Although she grew up lovingly cared for by some loyal slaves in the Todd household, she came to think of slavery as morally wrong. Although she had benefitted from it, she spoke out against it. Her cousin quotes Mary as saying, "It's all wrong... this selling human beings into slavery" (Helm 51). Although this conclusion about slavery seems obvious now, it took great courage for Mary, a southern aristocrat, to stand up for what she believed in those volatile times.

And finally, it seems that Mary valued very highly her relationships with a few important people in her life—people such as her two older sisters and a few female friends. She nurtured these friendships, as we see in her correspondence with her friend Mercy Levering, whom she met in Springfield in 1839, and then wrote to when Mercy moved back to Baltimore. She seemed to cultivate connections with people, not because they were important or potentially useful to her, but because she genuinely liked them.

What we have learned.

Among Mary Todd Lincoln's biographers, most agree with Ruth Painter Randall that Mary's growing up was relatively untroubled, that there was no hint of the erratic behavior that was to develop later on. Only Jean Baker implies that the loss of Mary's mother (when Mary was six) may have scarred her for life. This speculation, however, is merely that. She lost her mother, yes, but her warm relationships with her father, her Grandmother Parker, the slave Mammy, and her older sister Elizabeth all remained and continued to nourish her.

Indeed, if we did not know about Mary Todd Lincoln's later craziness, it would never occur to us to expect it. In the three existing letters that Mary wrote during her first 24 years, she sounds busy and happy. There is no trace of self-pity, no hint that she felt mistreated or unlucky. In two letters written much later she did refer to her childhood in what could be interpreted as a resentful way: her “early home was truly at a boarding school” (Turner 447), and her “desolate childhood” (Turner 588), but both these letters were written during a terribly difficult time of her life (1867 and 1871) when she was bitter about almost everything and lashing out at everyone. We simply have no facts to explain either of these comments.

During the first third of her life, then, Mary Todd Lincoln appeared to be healthy and attractive. There is no reason to believe that she did not feel as well as she looked. She behaved in accordance with her high social position and advanced education. It would appear that in herself she valued most her appearance and her future role as wife and mother, but that beyond herself she valued most intellect, culture, and friendship. This first third of Mary Todd Lincoln’s life was for her primarily a positive time.

Wife and Mother

This part of Mary Todd Lincoln’s life was the most public part. If we have seen a picture of her, it is most likely from this period. If we have an idea about what sort of person she was, it is most likely because we have read or heard something that she did or said during this time of her life. It was during this time that Mary Todd Lincoln both fulfilled her fondest dreams and suffered her most terrible losses. It was during this time that the craziness started, that the glaring contradictions began to accumulate. Yet throughout these 23 years, even when presiding in the White House, Mary Todd Lincoln was above all a wife and mother.

Few people noticed when Mary Todd married someone “beneath” her, someone without property or pedigree. Yet later when her husband was murdered, an entire nation watched her mourn. By the time her husband died, she had already lost two of her four children also. And she had lived through the Civil War in which she had loved ones fighting and dying on both sides. She began this period of her life in a boarding house in obscure but friendly Springfield, Illinois, and ended it in the White House in the more cosmopolitan, more dangerous Washington, D.C. This was, for Mary Todd Lincoln, a time of extremes.

How did she look?

She looked good. For most of this period Mary Todd Lincoln appeared healthy. She was pregnant four times and had four safe deliveries. Although she put on some weight, she did not become "bloated," as she put it, until later on. And as the Lincoln's social standing improved, so did Mary's wardrobe, enabling her always to look elegant in public.

A woman who as a child knew Mary Todd Lincoln recalled that:

> Mrs. Lincoln was a very good looking woman, and had very pretty manners. I can remember how beautifully she looked with a lavender and white parasol, and clothes and gloves and everything to match. (Goltz 50)

Even William Herndon, Abraham Lincoln's controversial law partner in Springfield, described Mary, whom he never liked, as "one of the belles of the town." He grudgingly admitted that she was "handsome and vivacious, affable and even charming in her manners" (Randall 120).

When Mary, a newcomer to Washington, became First Lady, most observers were favorably impressed. In 1860, a New York reporter described the comely Mrs. Lincoln who would, he predicted, adorn the White House:

> Whatever of awkwardness may be ascribed to her husband, there is none of it in her. On the contrary, she is quite a pattern of lady-like courtesy and polish. She converses with freedom and grace and is thoroughly AU FAIT in all the little amenities of society. (Kinnaird 65)

Another observer, the prominent James Harlan of Iowa, whose daughter later married Robert Lincoln, described the new First Lady:

> She was fair, of about medium height, but standing near her husband, by comparison seemed short. Her quiet, gentle manners and fine womanly bearing impressed everyone with the conviction that she as a well-educated, cultured lady, accustomed to the usages of society and with ability to take care of herself." (Kinnaird 77, Helm 167)

It seems, then, that in this second third of her life, as during the first, Mary Todd Lincoln appeared to the world around her as a physically healthy woman, well-mannered and well-dressed. Her body did not yet appear ravaged as it would later appear to be.

How did she feel?

It begins to be more difficult to understand how Mary Todd Lincoln felt during this time of her life, for she obviously wanted very much to feel well. Although she had many responsibilities, private and public, her responsibilities as wife and mother seemed to come first. Yet her biographers agree that her physical distress was increasing through these years. Her pain was not yet the main theme of her correspondence, but it was a recurring theme.

Unfortunately, we have very little of her correspondence from the first years of her period as wife and mother. This may have been partly because Mary, newly married, had to learn very quickly about the hard realities of daily life. Suddenly she had no servants to care for her. Instead, she herself sewed the clothes, cleaned the chimneys on the lamps, baked the bread, carried the water for washing clothes, cooked the supper, and soon also cared for the babies. By all accounts she, formerly of the leisured class, did this hard work willingly and well. At least there are no records of her complaints.

As the Lincolns moved up in the Springfield social world, there were also more social duties for Mary to attend to, so perhaps she had little time for correspondence. At any rate, we have no letter from her that was written near the time when her son Eddie died at age four. We know that she and Abraham nursed Eddie, day and night, for almost two months. We know that both parents were devastated, that Mary was especially distraught. Although she was soon pregnant again and her life remained at least outwardly the same as it had been, we can be sure that Mary's sadness about Eddie never completely went away.

We do know, however, from Mary's own words, that much later, when Robert left Springfield for distant Harvard, Mary missed him just as most of us miss our children when they go off to college. To a friend, in 1859, she wrote:

> I am feeling quite lonely, as Bob, left for College, in Boston, a few days since, and it almost appears, as if light & mirth, had departed with him. I will not see him for ten months, without I may next spring, go on to see him." (Turner 58)

It would appear at this point, then, that Mary Todd Lincoln felt about her children pretty much as we would expect a devoted mother to feel. Similarly, in 1861, when she moved into the White House, she sounded happy and excited about her new home, perhaps just as most of us would feel if we were moving in there today. She wrote to her good friend back in Springfield, inviting her to come visit the Lincoln family:

> This [the White House] is certainly a very charming spot & I have found many delightful acquaintances. Every evening our BLUE ROOM, is filled with the elite of the land. . . I want you to spend the month of May, with us. ...the drives round here are fine, and our carriage we find VERY LUXURIOUS. ... Be sure & bring your boys, with you, the pleasure grounds here, are exquisite. ...I am beginning to feel so perfectly at home, and enjoy everything so much. (Turner 81)

A few months later she wrote again to this friend, urging her to come soon for a visit and to bring along her young sons. It is clear that Mary missed her:

> Bring your boys with you, it will be more pleasant all around. I am going to take my boys with me, with a servant man, who will take charge, of your children also. ... I feel that I must have you with me. I wish, I could hand you over the magnificent bouquet, just sent to me, the magnolia is superb. (Turner 94)

We remember, of course, that a terrible war was going on, right at her doorstep, while Mary Todd Lincoln was in the White House. There is, however, very little about this war in her letters. We know from other people that she was deeply concerned about the war, that some of her own relatives died fighting the North, that she did what she could for the war effort in Washington, yet in her letters she sounded like most of us—concerned about her immediate family.

During this time she lost yet another son to illness—eleven-year-old Willie. More than two years after Willie's death, Mary wrote a sympathy letter to her friend who had also just lost a young son. From this letter we can tell very vividly how Mary felt about Willie, and how guilty she felt now that he was gone:

> I am very deeply attached to you..., yet since I last saw you, I have sometimes feared, that the DEEP WATERS, through which we have passed would overwhelm me. ... Willie, darling Boy! was always the idolized child, of the household. ... THE WORLD, has lost so much, of its charm. My position, requires my presence, where my heart is SO FAR from being. I know, YOU ARE better prepared than I was to pass through the fiery furnace of affliction. I had become, so wrapped up in the world, so devoted to our own political advancement that I thought of little else besides. ...how small & insignificant all worldly honors are, when we are THUS so severely tried. (Turner 188)

Physically also, Mary Todd Lincoln felt increasing pain in her life. Indeed, it is in this period that we can trace the beginnings of what was to be a dominant theme in Mary Todd Lincoln's life. Pain, sheer physical pain. From her early twenties on, she was plagued with headaches. The earliest reference to these headaches is in a letter from Abraham to Mary in 1848. At this time they had two small sons and Abraham was away much of the time with his work. He inquired about her headaches, which must have already been a problem for at least nine years.

> And you are entirely free from headache? This is good—considering it is the first Spring you have been free from it since we were acquainted. (Evans 38)

But she was not free from headache, nor from other pains. Indeed, a sentence from one of her letters written in 1861 could speak for the rest of her life: "The weather is so beautiful, why is it, that we cannot feel well" (Turner 106). It would seem that throughout the rest of her life Mary Todd Lincoln never again felt well. But her headaches were her most debilitating source of pain.

> Reached here last evening. Very tired and severe headache. 1863 (Turner 159)

> I was quite unable during several hours yesterday to leave my bed, owing to an intensely severe headache & although it has left me, yet I am feeling so weak this morning that I fear, that I shall be prevented from visiting the Hospitals today. 1864 (Turner 176)

> An intense headache, caused by driving out, in the heat of the day, deprived me of the pleasure of seeing. . . 1864 (Turner 177)

Perhaps it is not surprising that the presence of pain in her life left Mary Todd Lincoln sometimes feeling sorry for herself. This theme of self-pity was not before apparent in her life, but by the White House years, even though she was rich and famous, Mary Todd Lincoln increasingly felt that her lot was unbearably hard.

After Willie's death, Mary was desperate with grief. She did not seem able to pull herself together. Abraham hired a skilled nurse, taking her away from the wounded soldiers who needed her, and asked her to care for Mrs. Lincoln for a few weeks. This woman, Mrs. Pomroy, was 40 and had already buried a brother, a son, a daughter, and a husband. She sat alone with Mary for hours every day for three weeks. She said of Mrs. Lincoln:

> She says she is tired of being a slave to the world, and would live on bread and water if she could feel as happy as I do. (Boyden 79)

No doubt few people could see how Mary Todd Lincoln was in any way a "slave to the world," but that is the way she felt at least some of the time during the period of her life when she was working hard at being a good wife and a good mother.

Mary Todd Lincoln's terrible headaches may have been exacerbated by the two carriage accidents she had while she was living in Washington. More pain.

How did she feel? During these years Mary Todd Lincoln felt close to her husband and children, but physically she felt increasing pain accompanied by a good measure of self pity.

How did she behave?

The inconsistencies were creeping in. During these years Mary Todd Lincoln was almost two different people: one of them the devoted wife and mother and First Lady that she was much of the time and the other a temperamental, self-pitying, unpredictable woman who embarrassed her family. She was both. Remembering that she was often in pain, that she had very high standards for herself, let us see what her actions tell us. We are not judging her, but respectfully looking for patterns in her behavior.

Mary Todd Lincoln still appeared to others as a highly intelligent woman. She read a lot to her children, even when she must have had many other things to do. She kept up her lively correspondence throughout this period. And she relished the idea of being in the political thick of things in Washington. She became friends with Charles Sumner and apparently loved to discuss the issues of the day with other prominent visitors to the White House. Some of these visitors, of course, spoke French, and Mary could converse with them in their own language.

As Baker pointed out, many political wives of the time either chose not to participate actively in the social scene or were unable to do so because of ill health. Mary, however, was a beautifully dressed, gracious and captivating hostess at the White House even though she was often feeling bad. She determinedly organized and presided over White House dinners and receptions even when she was in pain. A visitor at one such reception, left alone with Mrs. Lincoln for a moment, was charmed. According to this gentleman she "ended with giving me a gracious invitation to repeat my visit and saying she would send me a bouquet. I came home entranced" (Baker 197).

Her reaching out to people took other forms also. She frequently visited Union soldiers in the hospitals, taking them flowers, donating turkeys for their Christmas dinners. Often she would sit with individual soldiers and read to them or write letters for them. In 1864, she wrote to the mother of the sick boy beside her:

> I am sitting by the side of your soldier boy. He has been quite sick, but is getting well. He tells me to say to you that he is all right. With respect for the mother of the young soldier.
>
> Mrs. Abraham Lincoln (Turner 179)

Early during this period of her life, unlike later on, Mary Todd Lincoln's sense of humor was still prominent. She had a characteristically witty way of observing the people around her. For example, in 1859, she commented about the "secret" pregnancy of a mutual friend:

> One of the seven wonders has taken place. Mrs. Dubois, has a daughter, born two or three days since. Until the last hour, NO ONE suspected her, as she looked smaller than she ever had done. (Turner 59)

Another example of Mary's wit was recorded by her friend Elizabeth Keckley who was Mary's seamstress and companion at the White House. (More about this remarkable friendship later. Elizabeth was a former slave who had purchased her own freedom and then developed a successful sewing business in Washington.) Apparently, First Lady Mary wanted to depart from custom and have three large receptions at the White House instead of a series of smaller, more costly state dinners. Besides, she could kill more birds with just three stones. Keckley quoted Mary, talking to Abraham, trying to convince him to accept her new plan:

> Public receptions are more democratic than stupid state dinners—are more in keeping with the spirit of the institutions of our country, as you would say if called upon to make a stump speech. (Keckley 97)

Abraham agreed.

A good example of Mary Todd Lincoln's quick humor involves a story. Apparently she and Abraham had visited the war front, near Washington, at Fort Stevens, and watched as the Union forces withstood a Rebel attack but did not then seize the advantage and counterattack. Instead, they let the Confederate Army escape. Mary blamed Secretary of War Stanton for this embarrassing military display. When Stanton later called on the Lincolns, he reportedly said to her, no doubt in jest, "I intend to have a full-length portrait of you painted, standing on the ramparts at Fort Stevens overlooking the fight." Few people, however, successfully tangled with Mary Todd Lincoln, and she quickly put him in his place:

> That is very well, and I can assure you of one thing, Mr. Secretary, if I had a few LADIES with me the Rebels would not have been permitted to get away as they did. (Kinnaird 82)

We can probably safely assume that Mr. Stanton had nothing more to say on this subject.

In addition to her intelligence, sociability, and wit, there is one other characteristic of Mary Todd Lincoln that her biographers agree on. Most people who knew her agreed that Mary's "maternal instinct was of the very essence of her being" (Randall 81). A later biographer wrote of Mary that, "It was with her children that Mrs. Lincoln is most attractive" (Wives 30). Miss Sprigg remembered that Mary was "the kind of woman whom children naturally liked and that she adored her own children" (Goltz 50). When she wrote to a friend about the birthday party she had for her son Willie, for example, she sounded like many a devoted mother:

> Speaking of BOYS, Willie's birthday [ninth] came off on the 21st of Dec. and as I had long promised him a CELEBRATION, it duly came off. Some 50 or 60 boys &

> girls attended the gala, you may believe I have come to the conclusion, that they are nonsensical affairs. However, I wish your boys, had been in their midst. (Turner 61)

There were some, however, who pointed out that although Mary was a devoted mother, she was also becoming erratic in her methods. According to Evans, Mary sometimes punished her boys:

> . . . even whipped them; at other times she permitted them unrestrained liberty; and still at other times her method lay between these extremes. She did not maintain uniformity in either her attitude or her method. (Evans 139)

We can say, perhaps, that few mothers or fathers maintain this uniformity Evans is talking about. Indeed, one of Mary Todd Lincoln's most sympathetic biographers did make excuses for her becoming a "nervous, overanxious mother:"

> Pregnancy, childbirth, household drudgery, and sick headaches were beginning to tell on this abnormally intense little woman. (Randall 118)

The point is not that we expect Mary Todd Lincoln to have been a consistently wonderful mother just because she was in the public eye. Rather, the point is that somewhere during the middle of this period of Mary Todd Lincoln's life something within her was changing. Suddenly her loving and scholarly biographers begin to reach for excuses for her, to describe her tactfully as "inconsistent" and "erratic." The point is that there was now something about Mary Todd Lincoln that needed to be explained.

Elizabeth Keckley was employed by Mrs. Lincoln, and was also her intimate friend during the White House years.

But even Keckley, a loyal supporter who tried to defend Mary Todd Lincoln's sometimes strange behavior, confessed that

> I never in my life saw a more peculiarly constituted woman. Search the world over, and you will not find her counterpart. (Keckley 182)

John Hay, one of Abraham Lincoln's two secretaries, faithfully kept a journal during his stay at the White House. He had frequent dealings with Mrs. Lincoln, and an entry from a dreary day in 1862 is fairly typical of his apparent opinion of his boss's wife, whom he often referred to as the Hell-cat:

> Things go on here about as usual. There is no fun at all. The Hell-cat is getting more Hell-cattical day by day. (Hay 41)

Another person who worked in the Lincoln White House was William Stoddard, who later (1890) wrote more kindly of Mrs. Lincoln's inconsistencies:

> It was not easy, at first, to understand why a lady who could be one day so kindly, so considerate, so generous, so thoughtful and so hopeful, could, upon another day, appear so unreasonable, so irritable, so despondent, so even niggardly, and so prone to see the dark, the wrong side of men and women and events. (Stoddard 62)

Clearly, by the time Mary Todd Lincoln was first lady, something was causing her behavior to be sometimes out of control. People who disliked her pointed to these times with relish, and people who liked her tried to explain them away. But clearly these unfortunate times were there.

Mrs. Pomroy, who nursed Mary Todd Lincoln in 1863, said something disturbing about Mary—something that will perhaps make more sense to us later on: "My heart yearns to see her seeking comfort in something besides these unstable pleasures" (Boyden 79). We are left to speculate what these "unstable pleasures" might have been. Let us remember that the woman who used this phrase was a skilled nurse who spent several weeks at Mary's bedside at a time when even Abraham was wondering what he was going to do with his unpredictable wife.

Sandburg, who admired Abraham Lincoln tremendously and did not wish to find flaws in Lincoln's mate, nevertheless had to mention the trouble with Mary—her increasing loss of control:

> The contrast between them [Abraham and Mary] which grew in the years was in temper or control. She grew more explosive; her outbursts came at more frequent intervals, were more desperate exhibitions, enacted in the presence of more important persons. Her physical resources and mental ability took on such added pathos from year to year that in a wide variety of ways many who met her referred to her as a "sad case." (Sandburg 63)

Indeed, every biographer of Mary Todd Lincoln has had to come to terms with her increasingly erratic behavior. Yet sometimes, as we have already seen, even during the White House years, Mary Todd Lincoln seemed fine. Then the next day she would be angry for no apparent reason. Randall, a kind biographer, put it bluntly:

> Mary would use stinging words one day and the next day, in a forgiving mood, words of high praise for the very same person she had derided. The bitter words would then be erased from her mind; what she did not realize was that

> the one who had been their target remembered. (Randall 154)

And then she would be nice again. Randall compared Mary Todd Lincoln to a foot soldier with a "secret lameness" (Randall 221), which was not always apparent to the people around her. If Mary had had an obvious handicap, such as blindness or a crippled limb, people would perhaps have been able to understand her. Increasingly the people around her sensed that something was wrong, but they didn't know what. A secret lameness is a kind way to put it.

What was it that the people around her saw? How did she appear to be losing control? What exactly did Mary Todd Lincoln do that baffled them? People around her saw two things mainly: her outbursts of temper and her outbursts of spending.

Who among us has not had an outburst of temper? We all, after all, know how it feels to be edgy, to be out of sorts, or to just plain lose it and blow up. But there are only a few of us for whom this tendency to explode would be listed, by everyone we know, as a major character trait. Nor was it a trait of the young Mary Todd Lincoln, who was sometimes bold and outspoken and willful, apparently, but never, to our knowledge described as temperamental, unpredictable, explosive, or erratic.

Already during the Springfield years, as a harried mother and a political wife in a frontier town, Mary Todd Lincoln was being called erratic. Evans said that during this time she suffered from "erratic nerves, wild, sudden rages of temper" (Evans 155). And the Turners, who collected her letters, also noted the unfortunate change that was apparent in Mary Todd Lincoln by 1850 (the time after Eddie's death):

> The humor and control that had sustained her in the past became increasingly submerged in fearfulness, self-indulgence, and in sudden outbursts of rage, often directed at her husband or a servant and occasionally overheard by the neighbors. (Turner 41)

During these outbursts, Abraham was compassionate, they said, because he knew that his wife was "powerless to help herself." And here we have the first mention of Mary's powerlessness over whatever this worsening trouble was. Randall also believed that Mary was not responsible for these outbursts, her "hysterical seizures:"

> It is a terrible thing for an adult woman to go into a frenzy in which she is not responsible for her words or actions. (Randall 122)

And it was a terrible thing. Whether as harried Springfield housewife or as famous first lady, it must have been extremely difficult for Mary to see that wary look in the eyes of the important people in her life as they tried to deal with her.

In the White House, Abraham told Mary's cousin that Mary's nerves had "gone to pieces," and her cousin was also alarmed that Mary had become so "nervous and wrought up" (Helm 225). And when we listen to some of Mary's words written in the fall of 1861, we do hear the bitchy (not a nineteenth-century word) tone as Mary wrote vindictively about her sister Ann:

> Poor unfortunate Ann, inasmuch as she possesses such a miserable disposition & so false a tongue. . . Even if Smith, [Ann's husband] succeeds in being a rich man, what advantage will it be to him, who has gained it in some cases most unjustly, and with such a woman, whom no

> one respects...[who] as a child & young girl, could not be outdone in falsehood. . . She is so seldom in my thoughts I have so much more, that is attractive, both in bodily presence, & my mind's eye, to interest me. (Turner 105)

Mary Todd Lincoln was becoming the kind of person who was easily angered, but it was hard to tell when this anger would erupt.

One famous example of her sudden anger happened in a very public way, just before the end of the war and not long before Abraham was shot. It was early 1865, and Mary and some others had gone to the front to join Abraham in a review of the about-to-be-victorious troops under General Grant. It was a time of pride, at last, for the Union forces, and on this warm spring day Mary Todd Lincoln was there to witness the ceremonies.

Accompanying Mrs. Lincoln and Mrs. Grant on this arduous, cross-country journey, was Adam Badeau, who 22 years later wrote a vivid account of Mary Todd Lincoln's two embarrassing outbursts. The first was in the carriage, when Mary heard someone say that another military wife was already with the men (including Abraham). Mary was enraged: "What do you mean by that, sir? Do you mean to say that she saw the President alone" (Badeau 10)?

When the others in the carriage tried to reassure her that there was no reason to be jealous, Mary only grew more angry, demanding that the driver stop the carriage right there and let her out, presumably so that she could charge right over to the woman and reprimand her. No doubt thinking this would be unseemly, Badeau did not stop the carriage, whereupon Mary grabbed the driver's arms and physically tried to force him to stop.

The second outburst was even worse when, the next day, Mary saw that another general's wife was riding near the

President. Mary's jealous rage "was beyond all bounds," and she was in a "frenzy of excitement." Mary insulted the bewildered woman and "called her vile names" and "stormed" at her until the poor woman burst into tears. "Everybody was shocked and horrified." And then to make matters even worse, Mary Todd Lincoln stormed at her husband right there in front of everybody, repeatedly attacking him, turning "on him like a tigress." All of this was for Badeau, and no doubt also for the others, a "hateful experience."

It must have been hateful for Mary as well. According to Badeau, in her "saner intervals" she regretted "the very acts she was at other times unable to control." Indeed, Mary spent the rest of her stay at City Point in seclusion. Her husband apologized for her, telling the others that she was unwell. But by then many people had witnessed the unpredictable temper of Mrs. Lincoln (Badeau 10).

In addition to such outbursts of temper, the world was also seeing in Mary Todd Lincoln strange outbursts of extravagance. Although she grew up with wealth, she never appeared as a young woman to be particularly concerned with money. Then during her early married years she had barely enough money to live on. But during the later Springfield years, the money theme, which would later become such an ugly and prominent one, began to flicker in Mary Todd Lincoln's life.

By 1856, according to Randall, Mary's "gathering intensity about spending was a mania" (Randall 156). While Abraham was away she bought an expensive carriage and built a large addition on their house. He was surprised. And by 1859, the records show that Mary Todd Lincoln had made extravagant purchases of silk and cashmere for her own wardrobe (Baker 156).

We will see, however, that Mary Todd Lincoln was never consistently extravagant. Rather, she puzzled the people around her by sometimes flagrantly wasting money and at other times behaving like a miser. Evans, the doctor who later looked back and tried to analyze Mary Todd Lincoln, said of her:

> Mrs. Lincoln, between 1861 and 1865, was most foolishly extravagant and at the same time decidedly near, close, or frugal. (Evans 311)

Stoddard, who worked in the White House, described an example of Mary Todd Lincoln's paradoxical attitude toward money. After a few hours of "extreme depression," she proposed to SELL the manure from the Executive Stables and also to cut off all spending for necessities in the household in order to save money. A week or two later, however, "no demand for undue economy" could be discovered in her (Stoddard 62).

Abraham Lincoln was apparently very much aware of his wife's erratic behavior with money. After all, he was the President of a country mired down in an expensive, debilitating war. Therefore, he:

> tried to keep a responsible person with her when he could, watched over her himself, and, when she spent government money in a way he disapproved, offered to make it up out of his own pocket. (Randall 316)

Abraham probably disapproved of the exorbitant sums of money Mary spent redecorating the White House, for instance. She ordered wallpaper from Paris, spent over $2,000 on carpet and curtains in one day, and personally visited the best stores in Philadelphia and New York (eleven shopping trips to New York!) (Baker 185). Lincoln certainly would have disapproved of his wife's buying herself a $1,000 camel hair shawl (Turner 88). According to Neely, her husband was furious:

> Lincoln exploded in anger at the spectacle of extravagance displayed by his wife while soldiers shivered without blankets, but Congress covered the possible scandal up by burying a supplemental appropriation amidst other legislation. (Neely 4)

Congress may have covered up her extravagance, but Mary Todd Lincoln was widely criticized, as we can well imagine, for spending this warring country's depleting dollars the way she did.

She would have been even more criticized, however, if people, including her husband, had known how far in debt Mary Todd Lincoln really was. She told her friend Elizabeth Keckley how important it was for Abraham to win his 1864 campaign for re-election to the presidency. There was more, she said, at stake in this election than her husband dreamed of:

> I have contracted large debts, of which he knows nothing, and which he will be unable to pay if he is defeated. (Keckley 149)

Mary went on to explain that, unbeknownst to her husband, she owed over $27,000, much of it to New York stores for her own personal wardrobe. This was the same Mary Todd Lincoln, tangled in debt, who had told this same Elizabeth Keckley only three years previously:

> I cannot afford to be extravagant. We are from the West, and are poor. (Keckley 85)

As we know, Abraham Lincoln won that election, but as we also know now, his wife had already purchased, just before the election, $1,000 worth of mourning clothes and $3,200 worth of jewelry (Turner 88, Neely 5, Randall 371). Clearly, her irrationality about money, her spurts of extravagance, were interfering with her life. Shopping had become a "kind of intoxication to her" (Randall 259).

Mary Todd Lincoln behaved during this middle period of her life in an increasingly erratic manner. Evans described her as:

> explosive, but reasonable, angry but tender, kind but miserly, cultivated yet crude, a composite of conflicting elements. (Ross 321)

Much of the time she still acted like the intelligent, sociable, humorous woman that she was, relishing her role as wife and mother and even First Lady. But some of the time, increasingly often, she was like another person—a woman who lost her temper a lot and sometimes went on spending sprees. By the end of this period of her life, it was clear to all those around her that there was something seriously wrong with Mrs. Lincoln.

What things did she value most?

In herself, Mary Todd Lincoln still seemed to value most highly her role as wife and mother. She still valued the appearance she presented to the world and paid much attention to her clothes—so much so that she ran up large debts.

But during this period of her life, perhaps because she had much physical pain, she also valued her health. It would almost seem that, because she was so focused on herself, in fact, she had less and less time to nurture friendship and to read and discuss politics.

And a new value had crept in—secrecy. Mary Todd Lincoln's secret debts and secret shopping trips and secret arrangements with some of the White House staff made her life extra complicated. There seemed to be a number of things she did not want her husband to know about.

We know that she valued her family, that she loved them very much. But something was interfering and making that love more selfish. For example, when Abraham suggested that their son Robert, who wanted very much to leave college and join the army, should be permitted to do so, Mary refused. They had already lost one son, she said, and she could not bear to sacrifice another. (She referred to Willie, who had died in childhood, not in war.) Her husband then pointed out that:

> many a poor mother has given up all her sons, and our son is not more dear to us than the sons of other people are to their mothers. (Keckley 121)

But Mary was adamant. She would not permit Robert to be exposed to danger in the field where his services were not required. Her husband's answer was:

> The services of every man who loves his country are required in this war. You should take a liberal instead of a selfish view of the question, mother. (Keckley 122)

They reached a compromise, and near the end of the war Robert was given a position of relative safety on General Grant's staff. Mary loved her husband and her son dearly, but this "selfish view" of hers was becoming more apparent.

It seems that by 1865, Mary Todd Lincoln, who was losing control, valued her health, which she must have felt slipping. She also valued her beloved family, especially her husband who protected her and comforted her during her "nervous spells." But she now had many secrets. The circle of things that she valued most in life was shrinking considerably and shifting in ways that she probably really regretted.

What we have learned.

During the middle period of Mary Todd Lincoln's life, she was proud to be a wife and mother and, eventually a first lady. Throughout this most public part of Mary's life she dressed well and carried out her duties even when she felt ill. She felt close to her husband and children, even fearfully clinging to them. But something—perhaps the persistent pain, perhaps the medicine for that pain—began to interfere with her life. Toward the end of this period in particular, her erratic behavior became obvious. She was still intelligent and gracious and witty sometimes, but other times she was quick to anger for no apparent reason and prone to spending unreasonable sums of money on things she didn't need. Although she clearly loved her family and longed to feel well again, her increasingly unpredictable behavior made her increasingly difficult for others to deal with.

Widowhood

Suddenly, horribly, Mary Todd Lincoln became a widow in 1865. She lost her husband, lost her steady income and all her connections in Washington. Suddenly, she and her two sons had to move out of their house so the new President could move in. This was only the grim beginning of the grim last period of Mary Todd Lincoln's life. For her it was a time of swirling sadness, confusion, and decline. She was tried in public for insanity and committed to a lunatic asylum, she lost another son, she rootlessly moved around, and she ended alone and unwell, apparently enjoying nothing.

This time when we ask our questions about how she looked and felt and acted and what she cared about, our answers will not be easy to hear. Sadly, for Mary Todd Lincoln things just fell apart.

How did she look?

She did not look well.

We have only two photographs of Mary Todd Lincoln taken during the last 17 years of her life–one taken in 1867, and the other in 1872. In both she is seated, unsmiling, wearing black widow's clothes, and in both she has a fuller, puffier face than she had in her earlier photographs. In 1935, Evans, the doctor, speculated about the causes of this puffiness (Evans 340).

Yet, according to Mary's own description of herself, written in October, 1867, she was not round and overweight at the beginning of her widowhood. She wrote to Elizabeth Keckley:

> You would not recognize me now. The glass shows me a pale, wretched, haggard face, and my dresses are like bags on me. (Turner 441)

Since her clothes, which would have been widow's clothes, were certainly not hanging on her in either of the existing photographs, we must assume that her weight fluctuated somewhat drastically during this period. Perhaps she lost a significant amount of weight but then regained it before the "puffy" period during which both photographs were taken.

By all accounts, however, a few years later Mary Todd Lincoln suddenly became very thin. In 1879, she wrote from France to her nephew describing the loss of her "great bloat":

> I enclose a card of my EXACT weight NEARLY a month ago—since then, as a matter of course many pounds of flesh have departed. HERE, ...I am now, just the weight I was, when we went to Wash in 1861—Therefore I may conclude, my great bloat has left me & I have returned to my natural size. (Turner 690)

By the next year when Mary returned to America, she appeared to be, at age 58, a feeble little old lady.

How did she feel?

During this last part of Mary Todd Lincoln's life, her focus was almost entirely on her emotional and physical pain. She felt terrible.

It is well known that she was devastated by the murder of her husband, that she was devastated again six years later by the death of her son Tad. Then, after her insanity trial, she became estranged from her only living son, Robert, and his family. All this emotional pain was exacerbated by her increasing paranoia about money.

What is less well known, however, is that during this part of her life Mary Todd Lincoln was also in much physical pain. Near the end of her life, she wrote some sad words that pretty much summed up the way she felt during most of her widowhood.

> It is a fearful thing to be ill, ALL THE TIME. (Turner 714)

Indeed, she often said that with all her pain, she felt much older than she really was. In August, 1865, she described herself as:

> broken hearted, and praying for death, to remove me, from a life, so full of agony—Each morning, on awakening, from my troubled slumbers, the utter impossibility of living another day, so wretched, appears to me, as an impossibility. (Turner 268)

And four years later, in Germany at age 50, she was still suffering:

> I am sitting up & that is all, for my limbs are as painful & unbending, as an old veteran of seventy, should be. (Turner 524)

She went on to say, with what was becoming characteristic self-pity:

> Death would be far more preferable to me, than my present life. (Turner 524)

Although few people knew Mary Todd Lincoln well during this period of her life, we have much evidence from Mary herself that she was in great physical pain during the last third of her life. She most frequently described the severe pain in her head, back, and limbs. Yet throughout these years she also suffered from chills, nervousness, biliousness, and sleeping problems; she also reported problems with coughing, urination, and impaired vision.

After Abraham's death, Mary remained sick in bed for forty days. When she finally left Washington by train late in May, 1865, she had, according to Elizabeth Keckley, one of her severe headaches and Elizabeth "bathed her temples" (Keckley 210). Let us try to imagine the cumulative effect of such severe headache pain as we listen to Mary's own words through these years:

> I am suffering, to day, with one, of my severe headaches... 1865 (Turner 304)
>
> Three days of each week, almost, I am incapable of any exertion, on account of my severe headaches. 1865 (Turner 316)
>
> Owing to an intense headache, I was unable to read your kind note of yesterday until this morning. 1867 (Turner 408)
>
> I am suffering with a fearful headache to day. 1867 (Turner 460)
>
> ...one of my most tiresome headaches. 1869 (Turner 519)
>
> I have been suffering for three days, with neuralgic headaches, pain in my limbs. 1869 (Turner 522)

> I was confined to my bed on yesterday, with a neuralgic headache—and am feeling very far from well to day. 1869 (Turner 528)

> Yet it [your letter] found me confined to my bed, with a neuralgic headache. 1869 (Turner 535)

> I am JUST AGAIN recovering from a severe attack of neuralgic headache. 1869 (Turner 537)

> I am just recovering from a severe attack of Neurlagea—in my head & limbs—accompanied by great indisposition, which has been my faithful companion for more than two weeks. 1869 (Neely 165)

> I suffered all night with Neuralgia—in the head & to day — write this in bed. Probably 1869 (Neely 168)

> Two days out of each week at LEAST, I am confined to my bed & often unable to raise my head—with headache. 1870 (Turner 541)

> I write you very hastily, whilst my head is throbbing with pain. 1871 (Turner 587)

Not only was Mary Todd Lincoln's head very often throbbing with pain, but the rest of her body also caused her frequent pain:

> I became so thoroughly chilled on yesterday that my limbs—ache with pain. 1866 (Turner 323)

> TO DAY, my WRISTS even, pain with neuralgia. 1869 (Turner 524)

> ...a great & burning pain in my spine. 1869 (Turner 535)

> To day, I am suffering so much with my back—at times I am racked with pain. 1870 (Turner 539)
>
> I have been quite ill, confined to my bed, for ten wearisome days—and now I am JUST ABLE, to creep about my room. A fearful cold, appeared to settle in my spine & I was unable to sit up, with the sharp, burning AGONY, in my back. 1870 (Turner 546)
>
> I was groaning with an ALMOST broken back—which is aching very badly at present. 1880 (Turner 695)
>
> ...sufferings of my back & left side. 1880 (Turner 699)
>
> I am suffering EVEN more than usual with my back to day. 1880 (Turner 701)
>
> I decline many callers, with painful sores & an aching back. 1881 (Turner 709)

Mary Todd Lincoln had other physical problems, which we will discuss in the closing chapter, but the most striking thing about her later years was her very real and persistent pain. She was forced to look at the world through the throbbing pain in her head, and she was forced to function with frequent racking pain in her back and limbs.

How did she behave?

Much of this time she acted like a crazy woman. Apparently Abraham's death was a terrible catalyst:

> Her husband's death had brought into permanent dominance all that was unappealing—even abnormal—in her nature. The sophisticated, flirtatious woman who had delighted in clever talk, high fashion, the theater, and the opera, had vanished overnight. In her place sat an aging creature, garbed in funereal black, drowning in waves of anxiety and self-pity. (Turner 238)

Or as one kindly biographer said of her,

> Certainly Mrs. Lincoln's chemistry was out of balance. (Ross 339)

Perhaps such an imbalance was what Mary Todd Lincoln's sister Elizabeth had in mind when she wrote to Robert Lincoln in 1875, after Mary had been committed to the insane asylum. Elizabeth, who comforted and cared for Mary, discreetly referred to the "peculiarities" of Mary's "whole life," which Mary's family had long been aware of. Elizabeth mentioned Mary's "malady," but unfortunately the paper on the letter is torn and it is impossible to know what following words Elizabeth used to explain "malady:"

> The painful excitements of the past years, ONLY ADDED to the malady [here the paper is torn away] apparent to her family for years, before the saddest events [trial and commitment] occurred. (Neely 62)

In plain language, many people around her thought that Mary Todd Lincoln was crazy.

But let us stop a minute. Was there no longer any trace of the intelligent, sociable, humorous woman, the good wife and mother? Did she really no longer act at all like what we have come to think of as the *real* Mary Todd Lincoln?

The answer is a sad one. The original Mary Todd Lincoln did seem most of the time to be buried somewhere inside the unpredictable widow whose behavior veered increasingly toward the confused and crazy.

Yet never consistently so. Her behavior was increasingly erratic, yet erratic nevertheless. Occasionally, sometimes quite unexpectedly, fragments of the old Mary Todd Lincoln were visible. We should note these fragments as we wade through the wash of her distress that dominated the close of her life.

She was still intelligent, of course, and Leonard Swett, the distinguished gentleman whose job it was to knock on Mrs. Lincoln's door, inform her of her insanity trial, and take her there, was well aware of her intelligence. A few days after the trial Swett wrote a remarkable account of his historic visit to Mary Todd Lincoln—remarkable because in his account she did not sound crazy at all. Rather, she sounded "ladylike," as he put it, and quite like her sharp, intelligent self. Swett told her that her friends all agreed that all her troubles had been too much for her and "produced mental disease." Mary was not fooled by this euphemism:

> "You mean to say I am crazy, then, do you?"
>
> "Yes," said I [Swett], "I regret to say that is what your friends all think."
>
> "I am much obliged to you," said she, "but I am abundantly able to take care of myself, and I don't need any aid from any such friends." (Davis papers 6)

Mary went with him to court, of course, for he politely threatened her with handcuffs, but throughout the trial, according to Swett's own account, she acted in an intelligent manner.

Another example of Mary Todd Lincoln's reasonable behavior is found in a letter she wrote to her sister Elizabeth after she was released from the asylum and legally declared sane once again. Mary's desire to live in Europe among strangers is certainly understandable:

> I cannot endure to meet my former friends, Lizzie. They will never cease to regard me as a lunatic, I feel it in their soothing manner. If I should say the moon is made of green cheese they would heartily and smilingly agree with me. I love you, but I cannot stay. I would be much less unhappy in the midst of strangers. (Helm 298)

Mary Todd Lincoln did indeed spend much of this part of her life "in the midst of strangers." For she may have still been intelligent, but she was no longer sociable. As she pushed important people in her life farther and farther away, she had fewer and fewer friends. According to Keckley, when Mary Todd Lincoln the widow left the White House for good, "there was scarcely a friend to tell her good-by" (Keckley 208). After her husband's death, she wandered, choosing not to settle down, not to return to Springfield where she could live near family and friends.

She went to Europe, but lived there pretty much as a recluse. Eventually she and Tad returned to America, but Tad soon died, leaving her even more distraught than before. She wandered again, behaving strangely, and then there was the trial and her confinement in the asylum, again among strangers.

After her release and a short stay with Elizabeth, she wandered in Europe again for four years. Even during the last year or so of her life, when she had returned to America and was based again at Elizabeth's house in Springfield, she spent a part of that time in New York City. She died in

Springfield, but she was apparently by then a rather mysterious, reclusive woman who had maintained social contact with almost no one.

And so we look back and see that the Mary Todd Lincoln we defined as intelligent, sociable, and humorous, only rarely exhibited these characteristics in the last period of her life. The woman with the keen mind for issues and politics no longer concerned herself with them. She apparently no longer read, no longer went to the theater. The woman who seemed to thrive most of her life as the "belle" of whatever ball she chose to create, now seemed almost to cringe in a corner of her own life. And the woman whose ready wit forced even her enemies to admire her was now, at age 46, too preoccupied most of the time to see much humor in anything.

But what of her role as wife and mother which she had always filled with honor and determination? Suddenly she was a wife no longer, of course, but in 1865, her sons Robert and Tad were ages 22 and 12. It would appear that Mary Todd Lincoln was no longer able to concentrate on her sons' welfare. This mother who had healthily and happily doted on her boys, by now was unable to get out of herself for long enough to help them very much.

There is little indication that Mary realized that Robert had lost his father, that Robert's education had been rudely interrupted, that he now was, in his own eyes, the man of the family, responsible for his young brother and his ailing mother. And because Mary was bereft and incapacitated after his father's death, it was Robert who summoned help for his mother, who attended his father's funeral without her, who supervised the packing of the household goods, and who finally cajoled his mother into leaving her bed of pain in President Johnson's White House to board the train for Chicago. At the same time, of course, he had to figure out a way to finish his education and carve out a career for himself without the help of his famous father.

Nor is there much evidence that Mary Todd Lincoln was able to focus on Tad's needs for very long. At the age of 12, Tad was apparently a likable boy but one with a speech problem and perhaps what we would today call a learning disability. He had suddenly lost his father, whom he adored, and he, too, had to move out of his house and travel to a strange city far away. His mother was too ill and grief-stricken even to get out of bed. She could not attend his father's funeral with him or accompany him when he testified at the trial of his father's murderer (one of the conspirators, John Suratt). Suddenly she told him they had no money. And she began dragging him around the country, then across the ocean where he had to go to a German school. Indeed, from age 12 until his death at age 18, Tad never went to the same school for more than one year. During his last illness, his mother was terribly upset, of course, but so upset that she could not even spend much time with him.

Although Mary Todd Lincoln loved her sons very much and wanted to care for them, after her husband's death she was increasingly unable to be the attentive mother she once was. Nor was she able to enjoy the logical extension of motherhood, being a grandmother. She sent gifts to Robert's baby Mary, but in her subsequent letters she did not refer to this child as an important person in her life. Indeed, Mary did not even mention the birth in 1873, of her only grandson, Robert's new baby, Abraham Lincoln, whom they called Jack. Nor the birth of Robert's third child, Jessie, two years later. Mary Todd Lincoln's own survival required so much of her that she had little energy left to give to others. We know that Mary Todd Lincoln did not intend to end her life this way. A remarkable, gifted, loving woman, she now acted angry, extravagant, and mentally unwell most of the time.

Mary Todd Lincoln was very angry with a growing list of people she increasingly distrusted: Herndon, Johnson, Grant, Congress, the French, the Chicago newspapers, the ungrateful American people. She was also angry with most of her own Todd family. According to Helm, after her husbands death:

> [Mary's] former good judgment had become impaired. Her sisters and other relatives who voiced to Mary their indignant protests, entreating her to curb her excitement and eccentricity, only incurred her anger and had become estranged from her. (Helm 265)

Thus when her husband was murdered, Mary turned not to her extensive family, but to Elizabeth Keckley, a former slave and her seamstress and friend, perhaps only friend, during those last White House years. "I consider you my best living friend," Mary wrote to Elizabeth in the fall of 1867 (Keckley 301). Yet within three years Mary had banished this friend also from her life, angrily dismissing her as the "colored historian." (This remarkable woman had published a sympathetic "inside" account of Mrs. Lincoln's infamous attempt, in 1867, to sell her own clothes to raise money.)

Mary Todd Lincoln also became angry with two of the most important people in her life: her dutiful son Robert and his wife Mary Harlan Lincoln (daughter of the Iowa senator). Their courtship and marriage had been encouraged by Mary, who seemed at first to love her prospective daughter-in-law. She wrote to a good friend:

> In regard to the proposed marriage of my son, it is the only sunbeam in my sad future. I have known & loved the

> young lady since her childhood, our families have been very intimate and as she recently & sweetly expressed herself to me—that she was only passing from one mother to another. ...I consider this marriage a great gain—A charming daughter will be my portion & one whom my idolized husband loved & admired, since she was very young. (Turner 482)

Mary attended their wedding and then wrote fondly to her new daughter-in-law from Europe:

> You know, you will always be my FIRST-LOVE of daughter-in-laws—I often tell Tad—that I can scarcely flatter myself he will ever marry to suit me, quite as well as dear Bob—has done. (Neely 168)

In 1869, she also suggested to her daughter-in-law that she go to Mary's house in Chicago and help herself to any of the things, such as lace, which Mary had stored there:

> Also take any lace of any description—for it is all yours—or any thing you see— Every thing is only getting soiled, by being laid aside— There are also needle worked kchfs with M L worked in them, which are pretty—do oblige me by considering me as a mother—for you are very dear to me, as a daughter. ANY THING & EVERY THING is yours— (Neely 153)

She repeated this generous offer, later suggesting that Mary Harlan Lincoln might especially like to use a tea set that Mary had stored there:

> There is a rose & white tea set with flower vases to match— which I think you would like at 375 [Mary's house in

> Chicago]—Never purchase any thing, which you can find there. (Neely 165)

And so for a long while everything was just fine between them, even when, in 1871, Mary and her ill son returned from Europe to Robert and Mary's house. Mary wrote warmly of her daughter-in-law:

> We are received with so much affection here and notwithstanding the confined limits of this charming little home my son Robert, who is all that is noble and good and his lovely little wife will not hear to our removal. ... I love my son's wife whom I have known since she was a child just as well as my own sons and her warm heart has always been mine. (Turner 588)

Yet something happened. By the time she came back to Chicago from Florida in 1875, Mary Todd Lincoln had become "violently angry" with Robert's wife, according to Robert. On at least one occasion Mary drove the servants out of the room "by her insulting remarks concerning their mistress & this in the presence of my little girl" (Neely 36). And Robert heard that his mother was even contemplating kidnapping his daughter, possibly to get her away from this same Mary Harlan Lincoln that Mary Todd Lincoln had once thought so highly of. The rupture in this relationship was never repaired. Mary Todd Lincoln stayed angry.

We can imagine that Mary Todd Lincoln's anger with her son Robert was even more painful for her. Robert was her first-born and only surviving child, and she had always depended on him. Then Robert arranged for her insanity trial and commitment (for reasons we will examine later) and Mary felt betrayed by him. She could not believe that her own dear son could "do this" to her. He had obviously and meticulously arranged the trial, almost a sham, so that he could legally put her away and take control of her financial affairs. She was angry. And she stayed angry with him, apparently, until he visited her a only a few months before her death.

Because of Mary's long-nurtured anger with her son, she said some pretty nasty things about him. But before we look at those angry words, let us remember that when Mary was in Europe the first time, she still felt close to Robert, who was "growing very much like his own dear father" (Turner 465). She wrote to her daughter-in-law, "Bob is just as kind & noble hearted as he can be." Robert destroyed many of his mother's letters, which he thought would make her sound crazy to posterity, but that one, in which she sounds very motherly indeed, he kept in what is now called the Insanity File.

After Mary Todd Lincoln's stay in the insane asylum, however, she called her kind and noble-hearted son a "monster of mankind," a bad son who had "cruelly persecuted" her (Baker 349). She wrote of Robert, revising family history:

> That wretched young man, but OLD in sin, has a fearful account, yet to render to his Maker! And God, does not allow, sin, to go unpunished. In our household, he was always trying to obtain the mastery, on all occasions—never daring of course to be insolent, to my amiable devoted children or myself, when my beloved husband, was near, it was a great relief to us all, when he was sent East to school, then we had a most loving peace—So different from our other sons—he was always persecuting them. (Turner 634)

These were harsh words, indeed, but perhaps the angriest words of all she wrote to Robert himself, demanding that he send back to her the many things she had given him, including paintings and silver tea sets and "other articles your wife appropriated." (We remember that all these things were freely given.) These were bitter, ugly words, accusing her own son of robbing her:

> Send me my laces, my diamonds, my jewelry—My unmade silks, white lace dress—double lace shawl & flounce, lace scarf—t blk lace shawls—one blk lace deep flounce, white lace sets 1/2 yd in width & eleven yards in length. I am now in constant receipt of letters, from my friends denouncing you in the bitterest terms, six letters from prominent respectable, Chicago people such as you do not associate with. . . Two prominent clergy men, have written me, since I saw you—and mention in their letters, that they think it advisable to offer up prayers for you in Church, on account of your wickedness against me and High Heaven. Send me all that I have written for, you have tried your game of robbery long enough. On yesterday, I received two telegrams from prominent Eastern lawyers. You have injured yourself, not me, by your wicked conduct.
> —Mrs. A. Lincoln (Turner 615)

And now this angry mother was alienated from her only living son. And from his children, her only grandchildren. If he felt angry back, as surely he must have, he left no record of it, and as was proper, kept it to himself.

In addition to acting angry much of the time, Mary Todd Lincoln also behaved in very grandiose ways about money. She was sometimes very generous, sometimes very grasping, but generally unpredictable, to one extreme or the other, with money.

She was generous to Anson Henry's widow in 1866, to Abraham's widowed mother in 1867 (sending her a kind letter and a gift), to Robert in 1871 (offering him half of her share of Tad's estate), to Robert's wife (giving her $2,000 for pretty new furniture and handsome curtains in time for Christmas—Neely 181), to her sister Frances whose husband had died and left her with little money ($600 for new carpets), and even toward the end to Jacob Bunn who was managing her financial affairs in America but having serious financial troubles of his own. She wrote of her trust in him in spite of his business problems:

> ...if I had FOUR times, as much as I now have, most willingly would I place it in your hands for safe keeping. (Turner 663)

These were the gestures of a generous woman.

There was also, however, a grasping side of Mary Todd Lincoln. After her husband's murder, she received much adverse publicity for her wrangling with Congress for more money. There is still much difference of opinion concerning just how far in debt she was when Abraham died (Elizabeth Keckley said $70,000!), exactly how much Lincoln's estate was, how much her income would then be, and how much she should have been given by the government. But there is no difference of opinion about the wrangling and arm-twisting and wheeling and dealing and guilt-dumping that went on in and around Congress for or against giving the martyr's crazy widow more money. Thus, much of the world began to see her as grasping.

Mary herself heightened this image by precipitating what we now call the Old Clothes Scandal. Suddenly widowed, she panicked about money and conceived a desperate plan whereby some businessmen of questionable motive would display many of the clothes which she had worn during the White House days and try to sell them for fancy prices. Mary, of course, was to get a nice cut of the profits. The trouble was that the proper folks of the day were horrified that Mary would stoop to sell her own clothes and try to make money from them. The proper folks wanted to look at the clothes, touch them and check the price tags, but of course they would never buy any of them! Many people thought that it served the grasping Mrs. Lincoln right that she made no profit from the humiliating Old Clothes Scandal. Most newspapers then portrayed Mary Todd Lincoln as shamelessly greedy.

Another aspect of Mary Todd Lincoln's often grandiose behavior with money was her compulsive shopping. In August, 1865, Mary bought 84 pairs of gloves from a Chicago store (Turner 275). At her insanity trial a major part of the evidence against her was the list of merchandise she had recently purchased but could not possibly use: $600 worth of lace curtains, $700 worth of jewelry, three watches costing $450, a bolt of silk for $200, and $200 worth of soaps and perfumes (Ross 308).

While at Batavia, where she had many trunks of clothes stored, Mary Todd Lincoln was permitted to go on shopping trips. After she left Batavia to live with her sister Elizabeth in Springfield, Elizabeth's husband wrote of Mary, whom he described as often "petulant":

> There is no doubt that her chief enjoyment consists in purchasing and storing. She is very secretive—errand boys go to her room—and the merchants disguise from me the extent of her mania. (Insanity file Jan. 16, 1876, Ninian to Robert)

Robert Lincoln said more than once that his mother was sane most of the time, with the one exception of money. Indeed, she did seem confused about money.

By this time, 1865, Mary Todd Lincoln seemed to be confused about other things as well. Many people apparently thought she was really insane, although most people, like Robert, found her only insane *some* of the time. Robert wrote to his uncle, after he had already had his mother arrested, tried, and committed for insanity:

> At the height of my mother's mental troubles she usually appeared to me personally to be perfectly sane. (Baker 330)

Yet Robert had hired a nurse and then later Pinkerton detectives to look after his mother during her wanderings. Robert also admitted to his aunt that during his mother's insanity trial he had discreetly permitted only a very few examples of his mother's bizarre behavior to be presented as evidence:

> I would be ashamed to put on paper an account of many of her insane acts—and I allowed to be introduced in evidence only so much as was necessary to establish the case. (Neely 37)

The evidence that he allowed to be introduced was that Mary Todd Lincoln was excessively nervous, had delusions, grieved uncontrollably, shopped compulsively, and made a public display of herself selling her old clothes.

Although Robert apparently did not believe his mother was insane all of the time, he did think she was "unmanageable" (Evans 217) and must be committed to an insane asylum. She was declared legally insane in May, 1875.

Much later, perhaps after Robert realized how futile his attempt to protect his mother had been, he admitted that the consulting doctors (none of whom was a specialist in mental disorders) had reached their diagnosis of insanity only orally, talking together about Mary Todd Lincoln, not to her. After this discussion, however, one of those doctors did write down his opinion:

> I am decidedly of the opinion that Mrs. Lincoln IS INSANE. The character of her insanity is such that she may, at times, appear perfectly sane in ordinary conversation; and yet she is constantly subject to such mental hallucinations as to render her entirely unsafe if left to herself. (Neely 31)

Other people were also troubled by Mrs. Lincoln's tendency to appear deranged at times. The Rev. N. W. Miner, for example, had known Mary Todd Lincoln most of her adult life. After her death, he tried in a Chicago newspaper to defend his friend's erratic behavior:

> Sometimes she was deranged, and this led her to do and say many strange things which were taken up by the press and she was severely criticised. But the reporters did not know they were criticising the words and acts of a woman who was not accountable for anything she either did or said. There were times, however, when her mind was sane on many subjects, and you could not detect in conversations with her anything that would lead you to suspect that it was impaired. (Chicago Tribune, April 21, 1888, p. 15)

The Turners, who thoughtfully compiled Mary Todd Lincoln's letters, were well aware of her "increasingly erratic behavior" in this last period of her life. They respected the insanity verdict because it represented the consensus of a number of honorable men, including Robert himself, but they could find no evidence in Mary's letters of insanity. From her letters they concluded that Mary Todd Lincoln was:

> irrational on, and obsessed by, the subject of money, that she could not control her compulsion to buy, that she was abnormally acquisitive. We can see that she often felt depressed, fearful, and persecuted, that she could be hysterical, vindictive, self-pitying, and self-deluding. She was not above stretching or abandoning the truth to serve her own purposes, however obscure. (Turner 614)

But not a lunatic, they said:

> Yet whatever else she has revealed of her mind and character in letters, she has, interestingly and ironically enough, refused to testify to her own madness. (Turner 614)

It is, of course, quite likely that any such letters in which Mary would "testify to her own madness," were destroyed by Robert.

The Chicago newspapers, however, did not hesitate to call Mrs. Abraham Lincoln insane, such as in these headlines:

> Mrs. Mary Lincoln, the Widow of the Late President, Adjudged Insane (Chicago Times, May 20, 1875)

> Mrs. Lincoln, Another Sad Chapter in the Life of the Demented Widow (Chicago Inter-Ocean, May 21, 1875)

During her insanity trial, Mary Todd Lincoln was apparently passive and appeared unmoved. A few hours after the trial, however, when she knew that the next day she would be taken to the insane asylum, Mary Todd Lincoln escaped from her guarded hotel room and went to the hotel pharmacy. There she ordered laudanum, it has been assumed, to commit suicide. Because the pharmacist did not want to give it to her, he told her to come back in a little while. Apparently desperate, she was not willing to wait and went down the street to another pharmacy, where that pharmacist, already warned, also did not give it to her. She then visited yet another pharmacist, was given fake laudanum, drank it immediately and came back for more. (In my third chapter this "suicide" attempt will be examined as something quite different indeed.)

The next day Mary Todd Lincoln was escorted to the insane asylum, where she was treated as a special patient (no doubt because of her high visibility). Almost four months later, thanks largely to the efforts of Myra Bradwell, one of the first women lawyers in the country, Mary was released. Her sister Elizabeth accepted Mary into her home in Springfield for a trial visit from the asylum. Gradually, Mary Todd Lincoln had a team. Her brother-in-law, Ninian Edwards, suddenly became one of her advocates, and Leonard Swett, who had assisted with Mary Todd Lincoln's arrest, surprisingly became her attorney in her second sanity trial. Thus, on June 15, 1876, a little more than one year after Mary Todd Lincoln had been declared insane, she was legally declared sane once again:

> wherein Mary Lincoln who was heretofore found to be insane and who is now alleged to be restored to reason, having heard the evidence in said case, find that the said Mary Lincoln is restored to reason and is capable to manage and control her estate. (Cook County Court Records)

Although few people who knew her apparently thought that Mary Todd Lincoln was really "restored to reason," they still weren't sure just how insane she was. Apparently they compromised so that she could be given back the control of her financial affairs and so that public criticism of Robert's mistreating his mother would cease.

Although Mary Todd Lincoln was declared sane again, probably few people really believed it because she still did not act very sane. And then she died, a difficult, lonely, reclusive, unhappy woman, much as she had lived the last years of her life.

How did Mary Todd Lincoln act during this last third of her life? She acted in an increasingly erratic manner, increasingly less like her former self, increasingly more like her crazy self: angry, extravagant, and mentally unwell.

What things did she value most?

At first glance it is difficult to tell what Mary Todd Lincoln valued most in the last part of her life.

It is easier to see what she no longer seemed to value very much at all. Her former values of family and society and culture had clearly faded by now. She had alienated herself from her immediate family, her son and his wife and their children. She isolated herself from her social peers. She traveled, but apparently only for escape or in search of yet another kind of medical treatment, and not for pleasure or stimulation. Her interest in politics, history, theater, literature, all seem to have vanished by now.

But there were some things that she did seem to value very highly indeed. She valued feeling good and living without physical pain. And she definitely valued money. And secrecy. Most of all, however, she must have valued the chemicals that she could buy and use and always have on hand to make her pain go away.

What we have learned.

The downward spiral is apparent. Mary Todd Lincoln, a bright and able young woman, slowly turned into an unpredictable, ill, and lonely old woman. She spent much of her life in pain, was weakened by poor health, and became increasingly erratic in her behavior. Her only living son had her committed to an insane asylum in order to control her strange antics, her extravagance with money, and her embarrassing outbursts.

II: Opiate Addiction in the Nineteenth Century

"Oh, doctor, shoot me quick!" pleaded the woman, begging for an injection. She was a morphine addict. She, in her fine, flowing gown, in her big house with people to wait upon her, was the "typical" drug addict of the late 1800s.

Most likely she had summoned her doctor because she was in pain and most likely he had introduced her to the miracle of morphine. Then when she kept on needing it because her pain returned, he kept on supplying it. At first both doctors and patients called this new form of opium the wonder drug, God's Own Medicine. (Many less potent forms of opium had been readily available for quite a while.) Finally, a pain reliever that worked!

It was not long, however, before they began to call morphine the demon-drug, the Judas of drugs. They soon noticed that sometimes it kissed its victims first, and then betrayed them (Courtwright, Dark 51). Over a century ago, this woman, and many other men and women like her, were victims of a devastating American epidemic, drug addiction.

Mary Todd Lincoln was one of these victims. When her family moved into the White House in 1861, she was 42 years old, the mother of three children, aged 8, 11, and 18. She had suffered from severe headaches for 20 years. She would no doubt have been using paregoric and laudanum to cope with her headaches during her Springfield years. Then, during her time in Washington and during the troubled years before her death in 1882, she had the best available medical care. The best medical care then, of course, depended heavily on opiates, particularly on morphine, to which so many people inadvertently became addicted.

But before we look closely at Mary Todd Lincoln's addiction, which we will do in the following chapter, let us examine the explosion of opiate addiction that was happening around her. What brought about such an explosion? Who were the victims and how did society react to them? More specifically, we will focus on five aspects of opiate addiction in the last half of the nineteenth century:

1. Availability of opiates.
2. Characteristics of the addicts.
3. Prevailing attitudes toward addiction.
4. Methods of treatment.
5. Stories of individual addicts.

This will be a background chapter, an attempt to set the stage.

Availability of Opiates

During and after the Civil War, medicinal opium was everywhere and almost everyone used it in some way or another. It was accessible to everyone. Although this sedative drug, a powerful pain-killer, had been known to healers for thousands of years, it was only in the 1800s that it became cheap and available in this country. Cheap and available, like aspirin is today.

Opium came in many forms and under many names. There were, for example, opium gums, powders, syrups, tablets, ointments, solutions, suppositories, and tinctures. Doctors prescribed opiates in medicines with many different names: laudanum, paregoric, morphine, codeine, and, by the very end of the century, heroin. Still other opiates, a multitude of them, were once as commonplace as Tums or Alka Selzer today: Dover's Powder, McMunn's Elixir, Darby's Carminative, Mother Bailey's Quieting Syrup, Ayer's Cherry Pectoral, Mrs. Winslow's Soothing Syrup, Magendie's Solution, Professor Hoff's Consumption Cure, Scotch Oats Essence, Godfrey's Cordial, Mother's Friend. Many of these names were household words which inspired trust.

All these opiates were available from the doctor himself (many doctors had their own drug cupboards), from the druggist by prescription (the prescriptions could be renewed indefinitely, and pharmacists often delivered), over the counter in patent medicines (many people could not afford to see a doctor), and by mail (which was cheap and handy for rural America). In 1878, a druggist said:

> At present it would not be difficult for a lunatic or a child to obtain at the drug stores all the opium he called for, provide he told a plausible story and had the money to pay for it. (Terry 97)

People used these various forms of opium to treat practically everything that bothered them: colic, diarrhea, cough, cholera, dysentery, alcoholism, headache, neuralgia, insanity, insomnia, rheumatism, morning sickness, menstrual pain, asthma, bronchitis, tuberculosis, nymphomania, sunstroke, hernia, seasickness. Just about everything. Some women even used opium for birth control. Some parents even, telling themselves they were giving their children tonic, quieted their children with regular doses of opiates. Most of these uses for opium resulted from the fact that it did two things very well. It considerably dried up body liquids (making it ease diarrhea and coughing), and it remarkably relieved pain (remember this was before aspirin and antibiotics).

And unwittingly, both parents and doctors sometimes used one opiate to treat withdrawal from another opiate. It was common to mistake withdrawal symptoms such as pains in the joints for the symptoms of another illness and therefore to relieve these symptoms with another opiate. This remedy, of course, just aggravated the basic addiction problem. One mother, who relied on Mrs. Winslow's Soothing Syrup to calm her daughter, was probably typical. "Why, she will get so mad if I don't give it to her, and scream and kick all morning" (Morgan, Drugs 38). And what busy mother does not want her child to be calm and content?

This, then, was the opium picture during most of the nineteenth century. The opiates were widely used by almost everybody for mostly medical purposes. There was some "recreational" use of opium, among the Chinese immigrants and also among people who considered themselves wild and artistic, but during this time most of the opium was initially used for medical reasons.

As a wonderful, all-purpose, every-day medicine, however, opium did have its drawbacks. Usually administered by mouth, it tasted bad, and it often made people nauseous. Sometimes it was administered through the skin, by massage or by cutting or blistering the skin and dropping it in, which, of course, hurt and left scars. Thus, people often had to suffer in order to get relief from their suffering.

About the middle of the century, however, two remarkable discoveries came along to enable opium to do its work more quickly and more comfortably. The first discovery was the isolation of morphine, an alkaloid of opium (codeine was another alkaloid, discovered later; then heroin, at the end of the century). Morphine was more powerful than plain opium, more concentrated, and easier for the doctor to control. Nor did it smell or taste so bad. But it was the power of morphine that was so important, for it was a powerful reliever of pain. By the time of the Civil War, morphine was plentiful, and most everyone was glad to have access to this modern miracle drug. Doctors discussed how and when to use it, but were generally unaware of addiction problems until the 1870s.

Then, just before the Civil War, a second remarkable technological discovery came to America. After all, morphine was wonderful, but it still had to be administered indirectly, that is, by mouth, or suppository, or by breaking the skin. When the hypodermic needle arrived from Scotland, however, it suddenly transformed the way morphine could be administered. It enabled the doctor (and eventually the patients themselves) to get the morphine more directly where it needed to go (the central nervous system). By the 1870s, every doctor had a hypodermic needle in his bag.

This new invention which brought quick and easy relief was welcomed by both patients and doctors. After an injection, the patient's pain stopped almost immediately, she felt calmed, and then she slept. Injected morphine brought heavenly relief. And the doctor was glad at last to be able to provide this relief (before this new technology a doctor could do little more than preside over suffering and hope for the best). With this new needle he could control the dose of morphine exactly, and he could stop the pain immediately. Also, because he often put in long days traveling great distances to visit his patients, now he could leave a syringe and some morphine with a patient and not need to make the journey back for several days. When he did return, he would certainly be welcomed.

As a result of these two steps forward, the introduction of the drug morphine and the discovery of the hypodermic needle, much human suffering was diminished. Unfortunately, another kind of human suffering increased. A number of people who used morphine found that they could not stop using it. By the late 1800s in America, there were alarming numbers of opiate addicts.

Characteristics of Addicts

Merely a few generations ago in this country the adult population had been brought up on the everyday use of opiates, and probably, just as we rely upon our wonderful antibiotic drugs, they relied upon their wonderful opiate drugs. Because these medicinal opiates were cheap and available and legal, millions of people used them. Indeed, one writer describes the United States during this time as being a "dope fiend's paradise" (Brecher 3).

During the second half of the century, the amount of opium imported legally into this paradise increased dramatically. An observer in 1878, for example, reported that between 1867 and 1876, the population of the United States increased 10 percent, while the importation of opium increased 70 percent (General 216). Similarly, the sale of opium in patent medicines increased at least seven times faster than the population increased. One person wrote in 1881 that in one large American city the population had, within 25 years, increased 59 percent, but the sale of morphine there had increased 1,100 per cent (Kane 6).

Given the wide availability of opiates, the inevitable result was a proliferation of addicts. Hundreds of thousands of them, by all accounts. And these addicts were everywhere, in all ways of life, in the country as well as the city. Even in Iowa, which was mostly very rural, the Iowa State Board of Health reported in 1885 that there were "over ten thousand people who are constantly under the influence of an opiate, and who are wholly unable by any effort of the will to break the habit" (Morgan, Yesterday's 41). Throughout America there were suffering addicts, many of them addicted to morphine.

Who were these addicts? Two-thirds of them were women. The majority of them were middle-class or upper-class women, middle-aged, and many of them the wives of prominent and educated men. These women, after all, could afford doctors (many people could not), and could take advantage of the best medicine the doctors could provide. A druggist in 1881 said that he used to make his laudanum by the gallon, but now made it by the barrel and that four-fifths of his customers were women (Morgan, Drugs 38).

In Chicago, where Mary Todd Lincoln lived, a study in 1880 showed that 72 per cent of the opium addicts there were women (Brecher 17). And in 1895, a recovering morphine addict put it plainly:

> A good woman is rarely overcome of alcohol, but hundreds of thousands of pure, virtuous, and intelligent wives and mothers in the land are under the pitiless thrall of opium. (Frisch 204)

That relatively few of these women were "overcome of alcohol" was probably because drinking alcohol was frowned upon—for women. "As a rule women take opiates and men, alcohol," a doctor noted in 1891 (Morgan, Drugs 40). Alcohol was less accessible to women than to men. And the opiates, which acted the same way as alcohol for "addictable" people, were more available to women because their doctors now knew what to give them for their "female troubles," such as morning sickness, childbirth pain, menstrual pain, as well as many other kinds of discomfort and nervousness which most doctors thought were related to a woman's delicate and different (from the male doctor's) insides. As a result, more women than men probably relied on the opiates, and consequently, more of them (but not all of them) became addicts.

They became addicts, most of them, by taking the medication given to them by their doctors. Their doctors (some of whom were also addicts) provided opiates for the real and imagined pains and distresses that we all encounter, and also prescribed them for all forms of severe pain. Indeed, by the end of the century some concerned voices were criticizing doctors for prescribing too much morphine for too long and for leaving supplies of it (and needles) with their patients. One doctor in 1894 spoke for many when he said that, concerning the extensive use of morphine, his profession was "wholly responsible for the loose and indiscriminate use of the drug" (Morgan, Drugs 39).

In defense of these doctors, however, we must remember that a doctor in the 1880's had far fewer pain relievers at his disposal than has a doctor today. When he could, he was glad to be able to calm and comfort his patients. By the late 1800s the doctor's image was improving in our society, and part of his new status as a savior was the result of the morphine he could dispense. It worked. And severe pain, as some of us know, is so terrible and so consuming that most of us, doctor or patient, would gratefully use anything that would bring relief. So doctors gave morphine, and people took it. Neither realized that some of them would not be able to stop taking it.

But some people could not stop taking it. As opiate addiction became a widespread problem, many people noticed the way these addicts behaved. The addict's behavior was increasingly erratic, increasingly unpredictable, and increasingly inconsistent with his normal behavior (Crothers 123). His behavior was eventually so erratic that people around him often thought he was crazy, or as Horace Day wrote in 1868, the addict was a "species of maniac," because:

> his views, his feelings, and his desires in relation to most things are peculiar, eccentric, and unlike those of other men, or of himself in a state of soundness. (Day 221)

But even the addict's craziness was not consistent, Day pointed out, for, "He is in a different sphere from other men, and in that sphere he is sane" (Day 221). By this he meant that the addict, however distorted his thinking could be, was remarkably shrewd and methodical when it came to procuring his drug and protecting his supply. (In this kind of writing during the nineteenth century it was proper to use the masculine pronoun for all of us. Today we can use whichever we please. And since most of the opiate addicts back then were women, I shall now use the feminine pronoun.)

By the turn of the century it became clear that opium, like alcohol, blunted the addict's senses, causing them to misinform her. She frequently miscalculated. She heard things that were not there sometimes. She misremembered. She saw things that others did not see. She misread other people's actions. She forgot things.

The result was that her personality gradually deteriorated (Terry 375). The people around her noticed her increasingly erratic behavior, her growing craziness. Many observers described this deterioration in terms of specific behaviors.

For example, the addict was increasingly withdrawn, forgetful, secretive, self-centered, and neglectful to her family. She was nervous, irritable, even sometimes unreasonably angry and suspicious. Her behavior was occasionally immoral, compulsive, even grandiose. And she acted as if she were ill much of the time. She was pale, had skin problems, sometimes saw or heard things that were not there. She often looked unkempt, had problems sleeping, and was frequently constipated. The addict's health, her work, her social life, and her family life were all clearly deteriorating as her innermost self crumbled.

We have not only these many descriptions of how the opiate addict behaved, but also we have descriptions of how she felt as she battled the drug that she had to have in order to survive. She was, after all, locked in a lethal battle for control. In the beginning of her relationship with the drug, she had been in control, and then as time went on, she often wasn't sure, for the drug deluded her. Then one day, to her horror, she realized that the drug was in control, and that her very survival was threatened by the very thing she had to have to survive.

In general, according to nineteenth-century sources, just as the key word for the way the addict behaved was *erratic*, the key word for the way she felt was *afraid*. Fear dominated her behavior. One researcher wrote of the addict:

> He fears death, he fears his ability to carry through the day's work; he is afraid of falling into poverty, and is obsessed by the fear that he will not sleep. (Terry 375)

One addict told how he even feared the very mention of the word opium. If he heard anyone say it, he would immediately leave the room, for fear that someone would mention his problem (Cobbe 60).

But most of the addict's fear was vague and huge, and she desperately tried to focus it on something (anything but the real cause, which she was unable to see, the drug). The result was that a host of negative feelings filled her. She felt guilty, nervous, anxious, and often angry. She felt depressed, worthless, and sorry for herself. Because she felt interest in nothing else but her drug, she felt lonely and isolated (Kane 49 and 19; Crothers 123).

And the addict often felt, as her addiction progressed, very sick. As she was trying ever harder to maintain the delicate balance (impossible now to achieve) between too much and too little of her opiate, she struggled increasingly with withdrawal. The agony was indescribable, one addict wrote, as every cell in his body raged because it was "emerging from the stupefying drunkenness of opium" (Cobbe 165). These withdrawal symptoms could be painful and exhausting. Yawning, sneezing, tearing, running nose. Vomiting and diarrhea. Chills and sweats. Aching bones and agonizing muscle spasms. Shaking, hallucinations, sleeplessness. Skin so sensitive that any touch would hurt it; hearing so sensitive that any normal sound would insult it. Thus, as the opiate addict's behavior became more and more erratic because she was feeling more and more fearful, she lived in increasing misery, caught in a deadly, downward spiral (Morgan, Drugs 69).

Not all users of opiates, however, became addicted to them (Lindesmith 47). Even though opiates were readily available, some people were more susceptible to them than others. Then, as now, it was not only the nature of the drug that was important, but also the nature of the person. Many people, for example, used laudanum to relieve daily pains, but some of these people, without ever intending to, became laudanum addicts. For then, as now, some people were more vulnerable than others. Just as opium varied in its addictiveness (morphine being, we believe, more addictive than paregoric, for example), so people varied in their "addictability." There were some people who used paregoric and became addicted, and there were some people who used morphine and did not become addicted.

There are many examples of people who used opiates but did not become addicted. Horace Day cites the anomalous case of a man who was 103 years old and had used opium for more than half a century without showing any symptoms of addiction (Day 248). A Boston researcher in 1888 examined the prescription recipes of hundreds of druggists, finding that many of these recipes contained morphine and were refilled again and again. But of all the people who used opiate medicines, he estimated that only 25 percent became addicts (Morgan, Yesterday's 183).

Apparently this trend holds true today with our most modern opiate, heroin. "The problem is," writes a present day expert, "that, while some persons can continue to use heroin occasionally, others cannot" (Courtwright, Addicts 63). In 1976, there were, for example, an estimated 7 million occasional heroin users in the United States, and only 700,000 addicts (Latimer 240). It would seem, then, that although there was an addiction epidemic in America during the late 1800s, many people who used opiates were immune to this disease.

In summary, then, by the late nineteenth century, many people were addicted to opiates. The majority of these addicts were middle or upper class women who took the drugs given to them by their doctors. There were so many addicts that addiction was recognized as a medical problem and observers were beginning to note typical addict behavior (erratic) and to realize that this behavior was caused by the addict's tremendous fear.

Prevailing Attitudes toward Addiction

Let us now look back as respectfully as we can and try to understand the attitudes toward addiction in late nineteenth-century America. These attitudes derived from what was generally known about addiction. It was known that addiction was a disease, that some people were more vulnerable to it than others, and that the sheer power of addiction was demonic. It was also known that opium and alcohol addictions were similar (although there was one important part of this similarity that had not yet become apparent), but the prevailing attitude toward a morphine addict was much more tolerant than the disgust often expressed for the town rummy.

Many doctors and addicts considered opiate addiction a serious disease. (A hundred years before Mary Todd Lincoln, Benjamin Rush had called alcoholism a disease, but during the nineteenth century the two branches of addiction, alcoholic and opiate, were not always seen as belonging to the same tree.) Horace Day wrote in 1868, that even an addict's best friends often criticize him for a "weakness" that is "not a crime but a disease" (Day 285).

The most important contribution to addiction literature, however, was a book by a German doctor, Edward Levinstein, translated into English in 1878. His title, *The Morbid Craving for Morphia*, may sound strange to us because we are unfamiliar with the original use of "morbid" to mean "diseased," but in his landmark book he described for his colleagues a new disease, "the uncontrollable desire of a person to use morphia as a stimulant and a tonic, and the diseased state of the system" that resulted (Parssinen 86).

Another doctor, in 1881, said, "The opium habit is a disease of the nervous system, and is not subject to control by the will" (Hubbard 2). And a New York City doctor in that same year wrote,

> I knew of one example where the wife, a young woman of eighteen, contracted the habit of using the drug subcutaneously, through the carelessness of her physician. The husband began then to use it himself, and to-day the two are separated, the wife partially insane, the husband a confirmed habitue and also an alcoholic drunkard. One who sees much of this disease meets with some very sad cases. (Kane 26)

About this same time, 1884, the Society for the Study and Cure of Inebriety was founded in England. It defined inebriety (either alcoholic or narcotic) as a disease like gout or epilepsy (Parssinen 87). And by the turn of the century, at least one expert was saying, "In drug addictions the condition of the patient is not mental, as is generally supposed, but physical" (Morgan, Yesterday's 196).

During the late 1800s many doctors also realized that some people were more vulnerable to this addiction disease than others. The poet Samuel Taylor Coleridge, himself a laudanum addict, wrote in the early 1800s that there were "two classes of temperament" to opium:

> those which are and those which are not preconformed to its power; those which genially expand to its temptations, and those which frostily exclude them. (Day 173)

The difference between the two, he said, was not a matter of will, but a matter of the person's "nervous organization," which doomed him either to yield to the drug or to resist it (Day 173).

Kane, the New York doctor, wrote in 1881 that although many people used opiates:

> Some seem to be so constituted that a single or a few doses of drugs of this nature light up in them an irresistible desire to continue their use. (???)

It is like putting a match to gunpowder to give them any form of opium. These people seem to have a "morbid craving for SOMETHING, exactly what is not known, until the narcotic is tried, and this morbid appetite is satisfied. . ." Any narcotic or other stimulant would, he said, satisfy this craving. It was just a matter of which one this predisposed person met first: alcohol, morphine, chloral, hashish, etc (Kane 33). In other words, some people, almost immediately, formed a special relationship with opium.

Some doctors began to point out that this affinity for opium (or vulnerability to addiction) ran in families. Many medical people believed that Coleridge's nervous constitution and Kane's morbid craving were inherited. A Philadelphia doctor wrote in 1902 that there was usually an "inherited predisposition" to any sort of inebriety, including opium intoxication. He believed that some parents pass "neuroses" on to their children.

> The children of such parents often find in morphine the first pleasurable sensations and relief from discomfort and pain. This drug seems to put them in a normal condition with a positive sense of physical satisfaction; life is full of zest; the mental and physical vigor seems perfect. The sense of strength is a delusion, to maintain which, larger doses are required, which in itself is a significant warning. (Crothers 70)

Many people, not just doctors, knew that certain families had addiction problems (a term which they probably did not use, preferring, “He’s just like his father.”). For example, among the important people in Abraham Lincoln’s life, addiction ran in the families of his step-mother, his wife, his law partner, and his murderer.

There was also the story of the Civil War soldier

> who became an opium addict because of a painful arm wound. He subsequently married, had two children, and managed until his death to conceal his addiction from his family. Nonetheless, his daughter became addicted to morphine following pregnancy and his son to morphine following a bout with drinking. (Courtwright, Dark 128)

Similarly, Dr. Calkins said that at the Binghamtom Asylum in New York, of 1406 patients there who had suffered delirium tremens, 980 of them had parents or grandparents who were drunkards. Calkins called this an “inheritance from a corrupted fountain” (Calkins, Appetite 117).

So, more than a hundred years ago they knew that addiction was a disease and that it often ran in families, but there was one more very vivid thing that they knew about it. They knew about the sheer and demonic power of addiction. It was a terrible kind of slavery which ended in insanity or death:

> this is a slavery the most damnable on earth; a bondage to a soulless, merciless tyrant; a captivity whose daylight is Despair and whose hope is Death. (Keeley 22)

This tyrant, then, became to the addicts:

> the only thing that, in increasing doses, can save them from the torment it has itself imposed; without it they are sunk into a living hell. (Kane 19)

Many addicts who recovered tried to tell the world what this living hell was like. The addict, said one, is in the "toils of a serpent as merciless as the boa-constrictor" (Lindesmith 118). Or he finds out too late, said another, that in falling prey to the addiction, "he has shouldered, Sinbad-like, a giant wearing the guise of a pigmy" (Calkins, Victims 30). Some addicts compared the addict needing his poisonous drug in order to "survive," to a starving man needing food. One addict said that this need is so great that it seems that "a weight, like a gigantic hand seems to be squeezing the naked brain as you would squeeze a sponge" (Morgan, Yesterday's 134). Another addict said that to be without his drug was worse suffering than being burned at the stake or buried alive (Morris 76).

Some addicts, like Coleridge, used the metaphor of the whirlpool—the terror they felt as they were helplessly sucked downward. And Coleridge tried to explain to his friends that it was useless for them to urge him to do something about himself. They might as well, he said, tell a man who was paralyzed in both arms to rub his arms briskly together to cure them (Day 152). Another addict, in 1868, said that he could not stop himself. You might as well, he said, tell a man on his deathbed to will himself not to die (Opium-eating 407).

But some addicts did escape the slavery to the demon drug, and one told how difficult this was: "you have to CLAW your way out over red-hot coals on your hands and knees" (What Shall 379).

Thus, the addicts who have left us their stories seem to agree that addiction is terrifying and total. It is important to remember, however, that not one of these addicts ever intended to become one.

How, then, did American society at the end of the century look upon these opiate addicts in their midst? The answer seems to be that they tolerated them because the opiate addicts to most people were not nearly so bad as the alcohol addicts. Americans then were much more concerned about alcohol than about other drugs (Courtwright, Addicts 2). Most people would have agreed with the writer who said in 1879 about drunkenness, "It is a monstrous habit, vice or malady, the fruitful source from which springs more than 90 per cent of all crime, misery, degradation and wretchedness with which the civilized world is cursed" (Dipsomania 3).

Alcohol addiction was terrible, but opium addiction was merely unfortunate. Unlike alcoholics, "The opium inebriate does not destroy his furniture, beat his wife, dash his child's head against the wall" (Parssinen 88). Alcoholics, who were often disheveled, disgusting men, were feared and hated, whereas morphine addicts, who were often quiet, respectable wives, were pitied and protected. Alcohol and morphine addiction were different things, most people believed, and there was not quite yet the stigma about drug addiction that we are now familiar with.

Yet even though people in general thought that alcohol addiction was worse than narcotic addiction, a few medical people were beginning to realize that the two were actually very similar. In 1878, Levinstein described some of these similarities, from the initial feelings even to the dreaded D.T.'s. He said that morphine not only relieved sleeplessness and pain, but also altered the:

> entire system. It produces a state of mental excitement that can only be compared to that produced by the use of alcohol. (Levinstein4)

He gave examples of this mental excitement that can result from both drugs:

> The temper is altered; depressed persons will become lively; to the fainting person it imparts strength; to the weakly it restores energy; the taciturn become eloquent; shy persons lose their bashfulness; and the consciousness of power and ability is greatly increased. (Levinstein 4)

This period of excitement, however, was inevitably followed by a deep despondency. At the turn of the century, another doctor wrote that "the use of alcohol is a narcomania of the same class as that of opium" (Crothers 341).

Levinstein also noticed another important characteristic of alcohol and opium. Not only did they produce similar effects in addicts, but they could also be used as substitutes for each other. He noticed that his patients often recovered from opiate addictions only to become drunkards:

> Even those who have recovered from the morbid craving for morphia retain a liking, and even an increased longing, for alcohol. They often, indeed, indulge in excessive drinking, and finding that the newly acquired passion is more injurious to them in their social relations than the craving for morphia, they try to amend by recurring to injections of this drug, thus again succumbing to their old enemy. (Levinstein 6)

Levinstein was almost identifying what would later be called cross addiction, the concept that once a person is addicted to one mood-altering drug, such as opium or alcohol, he is then also addicted to all the others as well. In fact, this understanding of cross addiction is probably one of the few things which we now think we know about addiction that informed people in the nineteenth century did not also know.

There were differences, of course, between opium and alcohol. Opium was cheaper and more respectable. It was easier for women to get—doctors willingly prescribed opiates, especially to women, the weaker sex, whereas a respectable woman would have had to rely on a man to purchase alcohol. Opium was a far better pain reliever than alcohol, and it was thought to be less physically damaging because it did not, like alcohol, go directly to all the major body organs. And, at least in the beginning stages of addiction, opium intoxication was easier to conceal than alcohol intoxication. But these differences were of far less importance than the striking similarities already noted by nineteenth-century writers between opium and alcohol addiction.

The attitude toward addiction, then, during the late nineteenth century was that it was a disease, often inherited, which had extraordinary power once it took hold. It was very similar to alcohol addiction in that it made its victims behave erratically, but, perhaps because its victims were mostly "respectable" people, opiate addiction was a bit more socially acceptable than alcohol addiction.

Methods of Treatment

As the opiate (particularly morphine) epidemic peaked in the 1890s, more and more people turned to the business of preventing and treating addiction. A number of books were published by doctors and former addicts. Magazines and newspapers offered many advertisements for cures and clinics, guaranteed remedies for morphine addiction. As there seemed to be more and more addicts, more and more voices spoke out about what should be done. Generally, they approached the problem, as we still do, from two directions, education and rehabilitation.

Some people, particularly recovering addicts who were still shuddering from the power of their addiction, suggested that education of all young people was essential. One such addict said in 1895:

> There should be general education of the young in the public schools, that they be warned in advance of the direful peril. (Cobbe 308)

Another young woman, miraculously recovering from her addiction, believed that the physicians who prescribed the opiates should do something to prevent people from becoming addicted to them. She wrote to her doctor in 1899, scolding him.

> You have it in your power to warn those who take laudanum now and then for toothache or headache, what an insidious thing it is, and how easily they may become the victims of it. ... You doctors know all the harm those drugs do,...and yet you do precious little to prevent it. (Confessions 550)

Few people heard such warnings, however, for then, as now, some people believed that opiate or alcohol addiction was just like tea or coffee or cigar addiction and that a person could, if he really wanted to, just quit (Morgan, Drugs 65). Or, as one angry morphine addict later said, the doctors just wanted him to "say NO," and everything would be all right (Frisch 205).

But whether sincere, thoughtful people in the nineteenth century believed that people needed education in the schools or from their doctors or no education at all other than plain common sense, their reasoning was the same: drugs (opiates) do awful things to people and if we consumers know just what these awful things are, we will avoid all these drugs. (We now think that it is not all people who suffer from addiction, but especially some people who are victims. And that these "some people" soon reach a point with an opiate or with alcohol where they are incapable of saying "no," no matter how much they know.)

Although there was beginning to be talk about education and prevention in the late nineteenth century, the real focus of the addiction problem was treatment. What should be done with all these addicts? The addict suffered terribly and brought much suffering to the people around her, so she desperately needed help. There seemed to be three basic questions about helping her. Should she get help on her own or go to a special place? Should she stop using her opiate all at once or taper off gradually? And were there other drugs that would cure her addiction?

To answer the first question, the addict or her family probably did two things. She bought a bottle of something (either by mail or from the druggist) that promised to cure her, or she went to her doctor. Or maybe eventually she did both. But let us assume that she first purchased a remedy, for she most likely considered this the cheapest, easiest, and most private way to solve her problem. So she answered an ad in her local paper or from the Sears Catalog. "Painless Cure for Morphine Habit, Satisfaction Guaranteed," it probably said. She sent some money to some place far away and waited anxiously for her Denarco or Opacura to come in the mail in a plain brown wrapper. When she received her cure, of course, she was unable to tell what was in it, for there was no labeling law in this country until 1906. She took her medicine in good faith.

And she was cheated, as were many, many others. A researcher in 1885 said, “the way these poor victims are fleeced by advertising quacks is pitiable, indeed” (Morgan, Yesterday’s 40). For the “cures” almost always contained the drug they claimed to cure her from. A bottled morphine cure, for example, often contained morphine. Or it contained other similar (similar in the sense that they would feed the addiction, not cure it) drugs such as bromides, cocaine, or alcohol (Morgan, Drugs 66). The result was, of course, that at first the addict did indeed feel she was breaking her morphine habit, for she was no longer injecting morphine into her body. She did not realize that she was getting the morphine (or something very similar) in her cure. Eventually, however, she met up with her nemesis, withdrawal, which she probably did not recognize as such, and in panic she usually retreated to her previous drug usage.

At this point the disheartened addict probably went to a doctor, who might have recommended baths or electric shock or gold therapy. Some doctors tried, as Coleridge’s doctor had done, to take patients into their own homes, but this was usually not successful. The addict, being an addict, would find a way to get to her drug. Thus, by the last decades of the century, most doctors realized that they must not only remove addicts from their familiar surroundings but also provide careful supervision during treatment. It followed, then, that doctors began to send their addict patients away to special places.

Many went to institutions for the criminal or insane. A Chicago doctor wrote in 1879 about how Belle Preston, once a “lady of fashion and high social standing, had fallen as far as opium and liquor could take her,” and ended at the Erring

Woman's Refuge (Dipsomania 25). The young woman, quoted before, who was recovering from laudanum dependency, wrote to her doctor in 1899, "I think you are right about a lunatic asylum being the only place for one to be cured of opium-eating" (Confessions 549). But she was wrong, for then, as now, few were cured. Many addicts, especially women addicts, ended in lunatic asylums and many died there. Or became lunatics.

One disgusted doctor, not wanting to send his prominent patient to such a place, wrote in 1867 "that the science and Christian charity of this country have perfected no scheme by which either inebriates or opium-eaters may be properly treated in a special institution of their own" (What Shall 380). But soon, by the early 1870s, there were asylums for inebriates, which treated both alcohol and opium addicts. By 1919 there were about one hundred of these asylums in the country (Morgan, Drugs 74). Unfortunately, some of them were "quack cure joints," which offered kickbacks to unscrupulous doctors who referred their addicted patients to them (Courtwright, Dark 51).

The second question about treating the addict, then, was whether she should stop taking the drug at once or taper off gradually. At first most doctors thought that the addict should stop completely, all at once, as this doctor pointed out in 1838:

> If wetting the feet produces pleurisy or lung fever, would any one advise that they be DRIED gradually, or be kept moderately wet for some time? ... If hot water blisters the surface, would you withdraw it cautiously, for fear of increasing the danger? (Grob 14)

During the 1870s and 1880s the prevalent thinking was that the addict should be deprived of her drug immediately. But because this method was difficult, painful, and sometimes dangerous, some doctors soon advocated a gradual reduction in dose of the addict's drug. As one addict wrote to the *New York Times* in 1878:

> If you were on the top of a six-storey building..., and wishing to come down to the street, would you jump out of the window, at the imminent risk of breaking your limbs, or maybe our neck, or would you come down by the stairs, step by step? (Morgan, Drugs 70)

The disadvantage of this approach, of course, was that the doctor became the policeman, always denying what the patient demanded.

Therefore, it was not long before a third method became fashionable, the method of withdrawing the opiate in a short time while substituting other drugs for "support." In 1880 one doctor suggested that cocaine be used as a substitute for opium and "taken as freely as the cravings of the system for opium may demand" (Morgan, Drugs 71). Others tried substituting cannabis, codeine, and even heroin.

Although these three methods of withdrawal appeared to be quite different, they actually had one important thing in common—they all relied on other mood-altering drugs, usually alcohol, which eased withdrawal symptoms and sometimes even sustained the addiction. In 1878 Levinstein, for example, one of the most famous proponents of the "cold turkey" method, explained that beside a patient's bed should be a table furnished with champagne, port wine, and brandy (Levinstein 113). Similarly, Kane, a New York doctor, an advocate of gradual deprivation, wrote in 1881 that if a patient was in danger of "collapse," he should be given wine freely, preferably sherry, or "whiskey hypodermically, three or four syringefuls at a time." He also recommended champagne, including a way to conserve it:

> There comes a little apparatus that can be screwed through the cork of the bottle, and by turning a faucet as much or as little can be drawn as wanted. It saves wine and keeps it from staling. (Kane 139)

So, yes, in answer to the third treatment question, some doctors and some patients and many entrepreneurs did believe that there were drugs that could cure addiction. None of these other drugs worked for very long, however, or for very many people. Most addicts who tried them became active addicts again. A famous Connecticut addiction doctor concluded that "the withdrawal of morphine is nearly always followed by the outbreak of an addiction to some other drug." As an unfortunate example, he cited a person who "was cured of alcoholic addiction and two years later was treated for morphinism, and still later suffered from the cocaine addiction; then he went back to alcohol, and finally died" (Crothers 104). It seems clear that most of these cures and treatments were contaminated by alcohol, which then, as now, many people did not recognize as a drug.

In summary, at the worst of the addiction epidemic in the late nineteenth century, some people were calling for prevention of addiction through education and even more people were offering treatment to addicts. Almost all of this treatment, whether in the form of quack remedies or institutional care, relied on other mood-altering drugs, particularly alcohol.

The result was that most treatment did not work, and by the turn of the century, some people were beginning to suggest still another approach to the problem—punishment. Dr. Crothers wrote in 1902 about the addict's behavior, "The alternations of sanity and insanity give encouragement to the theory of vice and the possibility of successful treatment by fear and punishment," but these only make things worse, he said, and "make the person more helpless" (Crothers 341). Apparently few people heeded his words, however, for in 1914 the Congress passed the Harrison Act, intended to deny addicts access to opiates and punish them if they found them illegally.

Stories of Individual Addicts

We have now viewed the general picture of opiate addiction in the late nineteenth century. So much for the panorama.

The big picture was, after all, made up of individuals, each one suffering. And unfortunately, few survived. Only a few escaped the slavery of addiction. Only a few looked the demon in the eye and then came back and tried to find the words, for the rest of us, that could tell us of their terror.

It seems a natural thing to talk about a narrow escape from death. To tell us how it happened, to tell us what it was like. To warn us. And also perhaps for the recovering addicts to comfort themselves, as if by putting something too terrible for any words, into words, they could somehow begin to understand it. Let us listen to the words of some who, unlike Mary Todd Lincoln, recovered from their addictions.

One young woman, still a student and living at home, studied hard and practiced her piano seven hours a day. She became addicted to laudanum, which at first helped her sleep. After she became well again, she wrote to her doctor in 1889:

> Perhaps you may remember a lady calling on you with her daughter about the middle of August, to ask you if there was any way of curing the habit of taking opium, which the girl had contracted. I, who write, am that same girl, and think you may perhaps be interested to hear how I got on. It is hateful to me to think of that horrible time, and one of my chief reasons for writing to you is to beg you to try and make known, by every means in your power, what a terrible thing opium-eating is. If people only knew of the consequences sure to follow on such a habit, of its insidiousness, and the difficulty of leaving it off, surely they would never touch it. (Confessions 546)

She went on to describe how awful she had become. She lost things and forgot things, even the names of good friends. She no longer cared about anything or anybody, and she became so deceitful that her family could no longer trust her. When they finally realized she was an addict:

> I had become so callous that I didn't feel the least shame. Even mother's grief did not affect me, I only felt irritated at her; this is an awful confession to have to make. (Confessions 547)

She was now grateful to her mother, she said, and emphasized again that the purpose of writing this letter was:

> the prevention of people getting into such a state as I was: if they were to know the state of moral idiocy to which they would in the end be brought, would they ever allow themselves to once begin the habit? They need not say to themselves, "Oh, we can stop it when we like;" opium takes away their power to do that. There can't be a more determined person than I am naturally, and what good did it do me! I determined a hundred times to stop it, but

> never succeeded, and at last I got that I didn't care a rap what became of me, all the reasoning and affection expended on me, being a mere waste of time and love. (Confessions 550)

Yet even as she urged her doctor to warn others, she remembered that he had indeed tried to warn her, but that she had then been indifferent to his words:

> Some of the horrid things you said are running in my mind, though I was so indifferent at the time, you might have said a good deal more without making any impression on me; even when you spoke about breaking mother's heart I didn't care. (Confessions 548)

And then, perhaps because she was young and had survived, she could let herself be a little flippant:

> Well, I wonder at myself being able to write such a long letter on a subject which is so repugnant to me that I try never even to think of it. I can hardly finish up in my usual style which is "hoping to see you again;" because I certainly don't hope so. (Confessions 550)

Whereas that young lady wanted to warn us, other addicts have focused more on just how they first got sucked into the whirlpool of addiction, as if, perhaps, a rational explanation (for something not rational) would somehow make it easier for them to understand. In 1881, one such addict, a lawyer from northern Illinois, pointed out that in the beginning the opium lured him gently, even as a friend. The friendship grew quite naturally:

> It did not make morphine seem an enemy whose fierceness must be placated, but a friend whose modest

> request there was no sufficient reason to refuse. It is in this way that the victim of the opium habit becomes a helpless captive before he is aware.
>
> The evil spirit of the drug hides its strength and touches the doomed one gently until it has made its grasp sure, then claws protrude from the soft hand and clutch the captive with a grip which he can have little hope of breaking. ...when I seemed to myself to be only toying with the monster and could escape from him when I would—I was, in fact, a slave almost from the first dose. The tiger was toying with ME—allowing me short runs of seeming escape—before it should make me feel the piercing of its fearful fangs. (Morgan, Yesterday's 117-18)

Usually the reason that the morphine (or other opiate) seemed such a natural thing to use was that it helped so much. It worked wonderfully well to relieve pain. Earlier in the nineteenth century, Samuel Taylor Coleridge, the famous English poet and addict, wrote how laudanum at first liberated him:

> I was seduced into the ACCURSED habit ignorantly. I had been almost bedridden for many months with swellings in my knees. In a medical journal I unhappily met with an account of a cure performed in a similar case, or what appeared to me so, by rubbing in of laudanum, at the same time taking a given dose internally. It acted like a charm, like a miracle! I recovered the use of my limbs, of my appetite, of my spirits, and this continued for near a fortnight. (Day 151)

In fact, he was so ecstatic about this panacea that he told all his friends about it and even carried a bottle around so he could dispense it to anyone else who was in pain. Then for a while he did not need his medicine. Eventually, however, his pain returned and he turned to his miracle remedy once again. Thus began the downward spiral, the "fatal whirlpool," from which he never escaped. Once he tried to explain to a concerned friend how trapped he felt:

> Conceive a poor miserable wretch, who for many years has been attempting to beat off pain by a constant recurrence to the vice that produces it. ...conceive whatever is most wretched, helpless, and hopeless, and you will form as tolerable a notion of my state as it is possible for a good man to have. (Day 161)

Still another addict, in 1874, who had battled neuralgia with morphine for several years, told how desperately he struggled against both the disease and the remedy. If he stopped the morphine, the pain came back:

> When does a man in severe and agonizing pain ever reflect? Although I suffered, suffered severely, when last I abandoned the use of the morphine, still I did not suffer as much from that cause as I was now suffering from neuralgic pain. I thought I was choosing the least of two evils. (Layard 699)

Indeed one doctor finally told him that as long as he took the morphine for neuralgia pain, he would continue to have that pain. His doctor apparently understood the addiction process, the increasingly impossible battle no longer to obliterate pain, but merely to balance the several pains.

Let us listen to another addict in 1895 describe the withdrawal pain that caused him to reach for his opiate again:

> The first work of the Judas drug is to double-lock the prison door of the will, so that successful struggle against the demoniac possession is impossible. During the subjection I fought nine times three hundred and sixty-five days against the diabolic master. Again and again the adversary seemed to be nearly overcome, the daily quantity having been reduced to a minimum, while in one titanic contest there was complete victory for five days; not one drop having entered the mouth in that time. At the end of these one hundred and twenty hours I was in a most deplorable condition. The entire surface of the body was pricked by invisible needles. If one who has felt the painful sensation of a single one will multiply that by ten million, he may dimly grasp the intensity of that form of suffering. All the muscles of the body were relaxed; there were copious watery discharges from mouth, nose, and eyes; the fingers seemed to be falling away from the hands, the hands from the wrists, and the knees smote together in an agony. Every joint of the body was racked with consuming deluge of sweat, which speedily dried and left the skin like parchment. Above all, the soul was oppressed with disquietude, the heart fluttered like a wounded bird, and the brain faltered from irresolution. Thus tortured by bodily inquisitorial demons, crazed by wild darting nerves, and devoured by apprehension of shapeless death, I held out my hand and, placing the poisoned chalice to the crackling lips, soon subsided into physical quiet and mental torpor. (Cobbe 28)

Certainly an addict suffering like this—desperately trying to balance her pain, inexorably being sucked ever downward into nothingness—certainly he or she behaved in ways that were increasingly difficult for others to understand. From the following descriptions of erratic addict behavior, we can imagine how frustrated and frantic an addict's family became. For example, Calkins tells us about Mrs. L., a wealthy widow, who was treated in 1854 for various problems. Her primary problem, however, which she did not consider a problem at all, was her addiction to laudanum. She steadfastly claimed that she did not take enough of the narcotic to hurt her, and that she took it only on her doctor's advice. Her servants also denied what was really happening to her:

> It was admitted by the domestics that now and then an overdose had been swallowed, but through some mistake purely, as perhaps in the measuring. (Calkins 78)

She also consumed a lot of ale, she admitted, and brandy "twice or thrice a day." And things got worse. She began to have more trouble getting started in the mornings, and she became increasingly forgetful. Sometimes she forgot where she was or insisted that she had been some place where she could not have been. She occasionally claimed to have heard directly from her dead husband. But the worst part was that her personality began to change in negative ways:

> If corrected in any way, she would manifest an utter intolerance of all contradiction, as that she herself ought to know about things, and who indeed should know better? The moral nature too had undergone change. Suspicious of near friends, and misconstruing the plainest acts, she would affirm or deny anything and everything, but believe nothing. Declarations of the most inconsistent, falsehoods the most palpable, she would one day asseverate to dispute them the rest. (Calkins 79)

More and more she needed coffee and snuff and brandy to restore her. She died in 1866.

Crothers tells us of another such unfortunate woman who reminds us, sadly, of Mary Todd Lincoln. In the late 1800s, morphine helped her, as it did so many others, in a crisis, but eventually it ensnared her:

> A widow, a leader in society and prominent for her intelligence and culture, was overwhelmed with grief at the death of her favorite son. The insomnia and suffering which followed were treated by the attending physician with morphin by needle. She seemed to recover and the morphin was abandoned by the physician. Probably from this time she continued its use secretly. (Crothers 123)

For five years this poor woman's family did not know what was causing her to be so "impulsive and erratic":

> After lying in bed for a day or two, she would have a period of an equal length of time in which she would be very energetic in religious work, then claim exhaustion and be secluded in her home for a time. Her conduct grew more and more inconsistent. She was forgetful of her promises and denied things which she had done a day or two previously; was suspicious of those about her, and at times manifested great irritability, then extreme penitence and sorrow. To her family she became more distant and uncertain—sometimes rarely speaking; then very effusive and anxious about their interests. She spent a great deal of time in her room . . . Her mental disturbances increased and her appearance grew more and more wretched. Finally she was taken to a sanatorium, when her real trouble was discovered. In all these years she had used morphin with the needle in small doses and had been able to conceal it from her family and friends. (Crothers 124)

Then, as now, this secrecy was a part of the addict's behavior. For no addict, most certainly, wants to be one. It becomes increasingly necessary for her to protect her supply, her supply that she wants no one else to know about, her supply that her survival seems so urgently to depend upon. What she must do to procure that supply and protect it, she *must* do. Better not to call attention to it. Better that no one know what she is resorting to. Better to keep pretending that everything is okay.

One addict in 1895 spoke candidly of his attempts to avoid making others suspicious. Any clerk in a present-day liquor store would probably be familiar with this scene:

> During seven years of the addiction a single drug store supplied the greater portion of the laudanum that I consumed. It now appears most ridiculous indeed, that, although visits were made there thrice weekly, I should have deemed it prudential to assure the proprietor, over and over again, that the toxic was to be used externally, adding a minute description of the symptoms of the suppositious malady. In the eagerness to convince the apothecary that such was the use to which the drug was to be applied, I would inveigh vigorously against poor fools who suffered themselves to get into the opium habit, vowing that no possible temptation could ever induce me to taste the dangerous narcotic. (Cobbe 57)

Another aspect of the addict's behavior was her despair. As the secret balancing of her pain became more and more consuming, more and more impossible, she felt hopeless. There often seemed no way out of this tangle but insanity or death:

> Mrs. Cheneworth hung herself in her own room, after retiring from the dancing party.

Her death was reported in 1868 by a fellow inmate in an Illinois insane asylum. (The writer was incarcerated there for her spiritualist beliefs.) Mrs. Cheneworth was an accomplished dancer and left a small child and an infant at home. She used the "facing of her dress" to hang herself:

> I cannot blame her for deliberately preferring death, to such a life as she has been experiencing in this Asylum. She has literally been driven to it by abuse.
>
> Her nerves were unstrung, and lost their natural tone by the influence of opium, that most deadly foe of nature, which evidently caused her insanity. (Packard 204)

It is a powerful thing that forces a young mother to take her own life. And indeed it is the sheer *power* of addiction that is the most striking element of every addict's story. The following four stories demonstrate this raw and terrible power.

The first story is about a young woman, age 25, who had been addicted to morphine for three or four years. She had repeatedly tried to stop, but with no success. Her procedure was to introduce morphine rectally with a small "acuminated glass syringe." Under her pillow she kept a vial of morphine powder, which she would mix with water and then fill her syringe. She had to inject the morphine several times a day, "abroad as well as at home; any by-place serving as a convenience, a side-room in a broker's office, or a nook in a secluded street" (Calkins 58). But one day she went out and forgot her powder:

> One day, in the height of the gold-excitement (Sept., 1869), the lady went down to Wall Street about ten o'clock in the morning, but without her usual supply which she in her hurry had left behind. Suddenly seized with overpowering tremors, she rushed into the first saloon she could find and swallowed a full tumbler of raw whiskey,

> and again a second after a little interval only, besides purchasing a bottle for use on the return home. (Calkins 57)

The doctor found her that evening "tremulous all over" and in great "mental perturbation." According to his instructions, she drank several pints of ale that night, and she went back to morphine, for she "must have it or die," she told her doctor. She had it and she died.

The second story, published in 1881, was about a wife who was being guarded by her husband and her sister, who refused—for her own good—to give her any morphine. The withdrawal was painful. "Her muscles twitched and contracted with such intensity as to throw her from chairs." The woman was desperate. After her husband went to sleep one bitter November night, she deceived her sister, who was left to watch her. Emptying her drinking water into her chamber pot, she asked her sister to please get her some more drinking water. It was sleeting outside, but while her sister went downstairs for more water, the woman

> weak from prolonged misery, with the curse of woman upon her, leaped from the window to the veranda, letting herself down to the ground. Like the slave in the dismal swamp, she was free, but with fearful surroundings. The sleet froze as it touched her only garment; but the opium horror was upon her, and she started across the lone prairie, sinking ankle deep in the freezing mud at every step.

Knowing that her husband would expect her to head for the village four miles away, and follow her there, this addict lady headed instead in the other direction to a village six miles away. The "opium horror" must have given her strength and cunning:

> The wife walked the lonely country road, facing the blinding sleet, her only garment heavy with ice. Arriving at the village, she awoke the druggist, a sensible gentleman and physician, who fully realized the terrible necessity that would drive a lady to such extremes, her disposition being modest and retiring; naturally possessing none of the characteristics likely to lead her to undertake a journey over the wild western prairie, clad in a night garment. (Hubbard 24-25)

The understanding druggist gave the woman some morphine to calm her while she waited for her husband who, not finding her in the nearer village, finally reached the second village and took her home.

A third story demonstrates the power that drives the addict to get to his drug, in spite of the efforts of his family to keep him from it:

> A very intelligent young man in Michigan lost both his legs in a railroad accident and during his long stay at the hospital had a morphine habit fastened upon him by his attendant physician.

When the young man returned home, his brother decided to stop this "slavery" and so forbade the village druggist and doctor to give him any more morphine. The addict had no legs and no morphine. Then, after enduring

> inexpressible torture, this poor wretch actually swung himself a distance of six blocks upon his hands to find the druggist and beg for pity. Finding him inexorable he dragged himself to the doctor's office; from which he was ruthlessly turned away. Racked by thousands of invisible fiends he then, still upon his hands, made his way to the

> depot, where, after some hours, which in his mortal agony seemed ages, a train arrived, and he traveled 250 miles before he found relief. (Cobbe 164)

The next story illustrating the sheer power of addiction is in the words of the suffering addict himself. He was addicted to morphine and injected the morphine hypodermically. His wife, thinking that she could get him to stop, kept finding and breaking his glass syringes. One night she stole his syringe from under his feather mattress while he was asleep. Suddenly awake, he knew that, even though he was severely crippled from rheumatism, he must somehow get to his horse and ride to town to buy another syringe. Fortunately, he did not have to risk the ride. On the floor of the barn he found the broken syringe:

> I actually crawled upon my belly to the stable, after hours of untold suffering, with the intention of mounting my horse—I am sure the task would have been impossible—when, to my infinite joy, I saw the instrument upon the ground. The needle had been broken off and with it a portion of the neck; but I seized it with delighted satisfaction, and, returning to my chamber, hastily dissolved a couple of tablets; after which I opened my knife and made an incision into the living flesh of the leg, inserting the uneven surface of the glass; repeating the operation until my blood was saturated with the morphine solution. (Cobbe 163)

No more stories. These are enough to show the power of addiction. The lady did not want to lift her elegant petticoats in the stockbroker's office. The farmer's wife in her nightgown did not want to walk six miles in an ice storm. The legless man did not want to drag himself by his hands from druggist to doctor begging for medicine. The crippled man did not want to jab the filthy, jagged glass into his own flesh. But they had to do these things. They had to.

The American opiate epidemic that peaked in the 1890's was the result of the easy availability of opiates and of the fact that then, as now, some people were more vulnerable to them than others were. The majority of the addicts were prosperous women who became addicted by taking medicine prescribed by their physicians. Although the addicts often tried to conceal their illness, they did not suffer the same contempt from society that alcohol addicts did, probably because most people did not yet realize that morphinism and alcoholism were symptoms of the same addiction disease. For this same reason, most treatment was unsuccessful because it involved substituting other drugs, thus fueling the basic problem. This concept of cross addiction was not generally understood.

Yet on a personal level, the stories of individual addicts from the late nineteenth century sound very much the same as the addict stories we hear today—stories of ever more erratic behavior, of a downward spiral of increasing desperation into insanity or death. The story of Mary Todd Lincoln.

III: The Addiction of Mary Todd Lincoln

Mary Todd Lincoln was a person in pain. Physical pain. Headache pain. The aching and throbbing dominated her life. Around, beside, and under the pain, she was a sister, a wife, a mother, a friend, but the pain, in her adult life, at least, was almost always there. It was the pain that defined her, the pain that confined her.

She lived with the kind of pain that you wake up under and spend the rest of the day trying to claw through. There was the pain, and then there was the job of being a mother and housekeeper and cook—all new jobs for Mary Todd Lincoln. We can imagine:

> *her head was hurting, but there were diapers to wash in the water that had to be carried to the wood stove that had to be tended and the children kept away from it and while the water heated her head was hurting and the bread had to be kneaded and the mud swept off the carpet with the straw broom while her head was hurting and the water boiling so the diapers could be stirred clean and hung heavy on the line outside while her head was hurting and new shirts for the baby would have to be sewn by the light of the lamp whose chimney must be cleaned while her head was hurting and the baby crying and the shopping waiting and the meat cooking and the flies seeking the meat smell and the children screaming while her head was hurting.*

And still, somehow, in and around the pain, Mary Todd Lincoln read her children stories. And prodded her husband to follow his political instincts. Through the pain she moved to foreign Washington, not a very nice town then, and through the pain she knew that the whole country was watching her manage that big white house. They watched her be the wife of our famous President, and they watched her witness the war that slashed apart her family as well as her country.

And we are still watching Mary Todd Lincoln. We watch and listen and try to understand what went wrong with her, what made her act crazy enough often enough to make her only son desperate enough to put her into an insane asylum.

Her pain is our clue. As a young married woman with a doctor brother-in-law, Mary would surely have tried anything to help her headache—any combination of available alcohol, paregoric, or laudanum. Later, having access to the very best medical care, Mary Todd Lincoln would certainly have been given laudanum, and eventually, morphine, for her pain. Neither she nor her doctors would have understood that she was vulnerable to such effective painkillers. Nor would they have at first realized that the proliferation of pains that Mary increasingly suffered were a direct result of her addiction to her pain medications. By the time they did realize what her "malady" (as her sister Elizabeth called it) was, by the time they connected this malady with her "unstable pleasures" (Boyden), it was too late.

It was too late when William Stoddard, who had known Mary Todd Lincoln in the White House, wrote in 1890: "It is easier to understand it all...after a few words from an eminent medical practitioner" (Stoddard 62). For by then Mary Todd Lincoln had already died the death of an opiate addict.

And it is too late now, of course, to help Mary Todd Lincoln. But it is not too late for us to understand what was really wrong with her. She died from the terminal illness of chemical addiction. Her sister and her son and her doctors must have eventually known this, but they were unable to help her. At best they hoped to protect this prominent lady from the increasing stigma of being an addict. By then, for a family on the nation's stage, even the stigma of being crazy was easier to bear.

Today, however, we know that this stigma is an empty one. We know that the chemical addict is sick, deathly sick, but not weak or bad. And today we permit our first ladies or anybody else to seek treatment for and try to recover from chemical addiction, or cancer, or any other terminal disease. Not that we always practice what we preach, of course. And not that we have made giant strides in understanding chemical addiction, but the fact remains that in 1875, there was for Mary Todd Lincoln, no Betty Ford Center.

Let us, then, look at Mary Todd Lincoln's life and death from the point of view of chemical addiction. Let us approach her addiction as we analyze chemical addiction in the Appendix, answering five basic questions:

1. Did she have a destructive relationship with mood altering drugs?
2. Was she genetically vulnerable to chemical addiction?
3. What mood-changing chemicals did she have access to?
4. In what ways did she behave like an addict?
5. What treatment was available to her?

Did She Have a Destructive Relationship with Mood Altering Drugs?

As we know, it is the very nature of a destructive relationship between a person and a drug that it be concealed. Concealed by the addict from the people who love her. And lovingly concealed by these very same people from the rest of the world. Even today when we understand that addiction, theoretically, is not a shameful thing, when we see it, many of us still attempt to hide it or to deny that it is there at all.

When Mary Todd Lincoln became addicted, then, the first instinct of her dutiful son Robert would have been to protect her, to prevent the rest of the world from finding out. Already in 1875, a man with powerful connections, Robert would have used all his resources to cover up the truth that his famous mother was an addict. His father's prominent friends and his mother's prominent family would all have agreed that her addiction must, at any cost, be concealed from newspapermen and the biographers who were already sifting through Lincoln material. They would have made sure that the written record never used the word addict and that it never mentioned specific drugs.

Historians have long been puzzled by two things that Robert Lincoln did. One was that he carefully engineered the insanity trial for his mother even though he knew that she was not really crazy. The other thing was that he, a man who revered history and honored his important parents, purposefully destroyed many of his mother's letters. Robert's motive for both of these actions, however, becomes quite clear when we see him as the loved one of an addict. He was merely trying to conceal, for her sake, as well as for her family's sake, his mother's addiction. It would, for

Robert Lincoln, be better that his mother be remembered as crazy with grief, even as just crazy, than that she be remembered as addicted to opiates.

But if Robert successfully concealed his mother's chemical addiction, how then do we know that it existed at all? We know by the way she behaved. With his mother's best interests in mind, Robert could have destroyed pharmacy records, altered hospital records, and arranged for only certain doctors to testify ever so discreetly (never mentioning medication or a specific diagnosis) at the trial. He could have destroyed any of Mary's letters that mentioned medication.

But he could not have destroyed all her letters, nor would he have wanted historians to accuse him of doing so. So it would have been natural to save some harmless (harmless to his mother's reputation) letters, for surely his mother's repeated references to headache, for example, would reveal nothing to posterity.

He was wrong. We respect his desire for privacy, but it now seems far kinder to remember his mother as a fine woman who died from chemical addiction than to remember her, as many still do, as the difficult and unstable wife whose sainted husband deserved better. And it seems far kinder also to remember Robert as the good son who tried valiantly to care for his ill mother, than as the ungrateful son who treated his mother badly.

What Robert could not foresee was that even with the deletions he left us in the record, we have more than enough information that Mary Todd Lincoln behaved like a classic addict. We don't need to know how often she took paregoric, who gave her laudanum first or what blend she preferred, how much brandy she was prescribed, or when she first took morphine. We have enough words from Mary herself to tell us that she felt like an addict and enough words from others to tell us that she behaved like one.

Still, we must be cautious. We are not the first to infer that Mary Todd Lincoln's erratic behavior might have been caused by chemical addiction. Evans, a physician, suspected bromides, but could find no evidence that she had been prescribed these. Apparently he was not aware that her hallucinations could have been caused by alcohol and chloral as well. And later, Baker also dismissed addiction, apparently believing the erroneous nineteenth-century reports that chloral was "harmless," and not understanding about cross addiction or the dangers of combining alcohol with chloral.

More recently, in 2003, Thomas F. Schwartz shares with us a newly-discovered letter written by Mary Todd Lincoln in 1874 (it is undated, but the other dated letters in this small group of six letters were all written in 1874, the year before Mary Todd Lincoln's insanity trial) to her doctor, Willis Danforth. Danforth was trained in gynecology and had earned quite a name for himself in Chicago. He also gave very damaging testimony during the trial. Here is the letter (Schwartz 135):

> Dr. Danforth,
>
> Please oblige me by sending about 4 more powders. I had a miserable night last night & took the 5 you left.
>
> What is to become of this excessive wakefulness, it is impossible for me to divine.
>
> Very truly,
> Mrs. Lincoln

This is one of the few letters we have left, after Robert destroyed so many, that mentions Mary's medicines. It is, according to Schwartz:

> the first written evidence we have of Lincoln's dependence on chloral hydrate. It also suggests that her 'insanity' as described by many, including Danforth, may have been drug-induced. (Schwartz 127)

It is not clear from this letter that Mary was addicted to chloral, but it is clear that she was addicted to something. Possibly she was using chloral to medicate some of the symptoms of her opiate addiction. And since the laudanum she must surely have taken had alcohol in it, the chloral would not have been a good thing to take at all, much less take regularly as Mary apparently did. The very drug-seeking tone of her letter is definitely addict-like.

But addiction is not something most people like to talk about. Although it is the first logical hypothesis to check out, it seems to be one that virtually all researchers want to avoid.

As recently as 2007, Jason Emerson concluded that, "the known facts strongly suggest Mary had no physical addiction to chloral hydrate or any other drug" (Emerson, 41). Emerson wants us to skip over the addiction argument, which cannot be proven, he says, and focus on his theory that Mary suffered from bipolar disorder.

Perhaps she did have bipolar disorder. Perhaps she did have untreated syphilis (Hirshhorn and Feldman). Indeed, Mary Todd Lincoln would not have been the first to medicate herself as best she could. Goodness knows, her migraines were enough to drive her to any solution. After all, most of us medicate ourselves with what we have available, and when our efforts work, we are pleased. When they don't, we go to the doctor again. And again.

As Clinton gently says in her newest biography of Mary Todd Lincoln, "it is not so far-fetched that Mrs. Lincoln's behavior might have been altered through her chemical intake" (Clinton 305).

In addiction work, however, there is a maxim, that the addiction, once it is identified, must be focused on first. Often there is another illness present also, and it cannot be ignored, but the addiction must be treated immediately. For the addiction muddies all waters. Once the addiction symptoms are relieved, we can see more clearly what symptoms remain and assume that they result from the other disease. Thus, the term *dual diagnosis* has become very common: a person suffers from addiction *and* depression or addiction *and* bipolar disorder. There are many other common combinations. But it is the addiction that must be ferreted out first.

Most of the historians who have studied Mary Todd Lincoln are not familiar with the behavior profile of the chemical addict. Ask any addict on the street, however, about Mary's being fine one day and awful the next, about her gulping down what she thought was laudanum, about her begging for chloral, about her fits of temper, about her dealings with "shady" characters, about her seeing things that nobody else sees, about everybody being after her for having changed, about feeling terrible, about seeing that look in other people's eyes that makes you ashamed.

"Been there," they will most likely say.

For now, until we answer the remaining four questions, let us say that Mary Todd Lincoln had a destructive relationship with mood-changing chemicals. She spent much of her adult life in pain, and she had access to the best medical treatment in the United States and Europe. In her later years, she increasingly moved around in search of new medical treatment that would relieve her pain. Most certainly she would have been given many different variations of mood-changing drugs, none of which apparently worked for long.

Was She Genetically Vulnerable to Chemical Addiction?

Yes. We do know that chemical addiction runs in families, and there is ample evidence of it in Mary Todd Lincoln's family. She had five full siblings. Two of them were addicts: Levi and George. One other, Ann, may well have been, but we have less information about her.

Mary Todd Lincoln's family on both sides was Scots Irish. Her mother, Eliza Parker, married Robert Todd and they had six children who survived infancy. Eliza died in childbirth when Mary was six years old, leaving the six young children with Robert, who soon married again and had eight more children (plus one who died in infancy) with this wife, Betsey.

Dr. Evans, who published his findings in 1932, investigated both these families, the children of Eliza (including our Mary) and the children of Betsey. He asked about their idiosyncrasies, how they fit in their communities, whether any of them were insane or used drugs (including alcohol) excessively. His conclusion was that all of these things happened much more to Eliza's children than to Betsey's (Evans 52). He saw a definite trend toward "abnormal personality" in Mary Todd Lincoln's family.

Furthermore, he concluded that this tendency toward abnormality was inherited (Evans 317).

We must remember that Evans wrote in 1932, before the American medical profession recognized chemical addiction as a disease, the vulnerability to which is inherited. He wrote before Alcoholics Anonymous was born, before his colleagues recognized the concept of cross addiction.

Evans's careful searching has provided us with much of what we know about Mary Todd Lincoln's two brothers, both addicts. Her brother Levi Todd, born a year after Mary, was the eldest son in this very prominent family. At first he seemed to succeed. He became treasurer for the city of Lexington, Kentucky, and managed some of his father's extensive business holdings. Then, however, his life began to fall apart. He initiated a vengeful lawsuit against members of his own family, his wife divorced him, and he died destitute at age 45. Evans said of Levi Todd:

> He seems to have fallen out with everyone. He used whisky to excess, and possibly other drugs. Abandoned by his former friends, at enmity with his stepmother, he moved away from Lexington and died, in 1865, in Franklin County; whereupon his stepmother claimed the remains of the almost friendless man, brought them to Lexington, and had them buried by the side of his father. [She did not, however, mark his grave.] (Evans 48)

Of course, we now know the tragic importance of Levi Todd's excessive use of whisky and other drugs. From this distance we can see that his disease destroyed Levi Todd, that the most unhappy details of his story resulted from his chemical addiction. We even have his wife's testimony. In 1859, when divorce was not common and most certainly when divorce initiated by the wife was not common, his wife,

Louisa Todd, filed for divorce from Levi, father of their four children. In the suit she charged that her husband had "a confirmed habit of drunkenness," that he was wasting his inheritance and not providing for his family, and that he was cruel and inhuman and completely unfit to be a father to his children (Evans 48). Louisa was granted the divorce.

Stephen Berry calls Levi Todd the "town drunk," who drank himself to death. (Berry 173) Near the end of his life, Levi wrote a typical addict appeal to Mary and Abraham, begging them for money, assuring them he would pay it back. What's more, he promised, with the grandiosity of a suffering addict, to vote for Abraham next time and bring lots of other voters with him.

Evans also sought information about Mary Todd Lincoln's other brother, George Rogers Clark Todd. The youngest of the first six Todds, George grew up mostly with the second of his father's families. He apparently did not get along with any of the Todds very well, however, and moved away. A physician, he served with the Confederate army during the war, and afterward practiced in Barnwell, South Carolina, where he was a competent doctor, but a difficult man. He married twice, became estranged from his only son, and committed suicide. Another doctor in Barnwell wrote to Evans that George Todd was very bright, but also peculiar, eccentric, and generally not agreeable. And that he "drank whisky to excess" (Evans 49).

George Todd's attorney wrote of George:

> He was of small build, florid of countenance. . . He took no pains to conceal his dislike for those who had incurred his displeasure and he had even been known to withdraw himself from a company when one whom he disliked appeared. The old doctor refused to consort with his own contemporaries to any great extent. After the death of his

> wife he lived alone and was given to moods of deep melancholy. Doctor Todd's only child, a son, was a disappointment to him. This son, evidently afflicted with "wanderlust," left Barnwell and went out west. After his father died he returned to Barnwell and recovered the property which his father had willed to others, but who gave it to the lawful heir as his right. He sold this property and again went away, never to be heard of again. (Evans 50)

Mary Todd Lincoln's brother George had a florid complexion, a difficult personality. He drank whisky to excess, isolated himself from others and then killed himself (chloroform). From this information we can assume that he too was addicted to alcohol. As a doctor with ready access to other drugs, he may well have used them also.

Of Mary Todd Lincoln's younger sister Ann, Evans said that a reliable person described her as "quick tempered and vituperative." He concluded that Ann definitely had a difficult personality, very much like Mary's, and that "part of her difficult and peculiar personality was inherited by some of her descendants" (Evans 47). This bit of information is not enough to tell us about Ann's use of chemicals, of course.

Furthermore, it was widely believed that Mary's half brother, David Todd, the infamous abuser of Union prisoners, according to many reports, was also dependent on alcohol (Berry 20).

As we might expect, not all of Mary Todd Lincoln's brothers and sisters showed evidence of inheriting this vulnerability to addiction. Frances, one year older than Mary, was never described as difficult or abnormal, although she married a promising druggist who became financially unstable and then an invalid (perhaps an addict also?). The eldest sister, Elizabeth, married well and became sort of the family caretaker, whom the others turned to in times of trouble. Although she does not seem to have been an addict herself, in a letter she wrote to Robert Lincoln, there is some indication of possible addiction (insanity?) in her daughter:

> Insanity, although a new feature, in our family history, first appeared within my knowledge, in the case of my own daughter, at the early age of thirteen—for six months, she was so decidedly flighty, as to be closely guarded—her back from irritants is scarred at length—At the birth of each child, the same symptoms were shown, and severely felt, particularly by her husband, and myself—At no time, has she ever been natural in her demeanor—God pity those who are the victims—and who are the anxious sufferers in such terrible afflictions! (Neely 66)

The scars on the young woman's back were quite possibly from opium treatments. Furthermore, at the birth of each child she would probably have been given opiates for pain. Elizabeth, however, may not have connected the opium with the abnormal behavior, and she probably did not then connect her daughter's suffering with the suffering and tragic death of her brother Levi ten years earlier. We do not, of course, have enough information about Elizabeth's daughter (none of her letters, no descriptions of her other than her mother's). Perhaps because she did not marry one of our presidents, we cannot be sure, but it is certainly possible that her affliction was addiction.

In Mary Todd Lincoln's family it is difficult for us to investigate farther back than her brothers and sisters. But no further investigation is necessary. The fact that addiction is present in at least two of her five full siblings is strong indication that she too was vulnerable to chemical addiction.

Although she did not know it, Mary Todd Lincoln was in grave danger.

What Mood-Changing Chemicals Did She Have Access To?

Alcohol, paregoric, laudanum (alcohol and opium), chloral, and morphine–these mood-changing chemicals would almost certainly have been given to Mary Todd Lincoln by her doctors. She also, of course, had access to the myriad ordinary medicines containing alcohol and or opiates.

At this point it might help us to remember that today when an active chemical addict enters a rehabilitation facility, he or she is permitted to have in possession no medicines, not even aspirin or athlete's foot salve. No hair spray. No mouthwash. No aftershave or cologne. The reason for this strictly-enforced rule is that many of these chemical concoctions can trigger and feed a chemical addiction, no matter what chemical the addict originally preferred. In other words, when he has to, an addict substitutes. Or he even substitutes sometimes when he doesn't have to because it gives him the illusion of control: "I won't drink this weekend, but that doesn't mean I can't smoke a little pot."

Mary Todd Lincoln would no doubt have avoided whiskey, for she knew that was what had ruined her brother Levi. But would she have realized that the cough syrup or the brandy or the paregoric or the laudanum or the morphine that her doctor provided her were just as dangerous, especially for her? Most likely not. Yet to Mary Todd

Lincoln, genetically vulnerable to addiction, all these were addictive–and interchangeable.

We have none of Mary Todd Lincoln's empty bottles, no rusty hypodermic needle that she hid away. Nor do we now need that kind of evidence. It is just that kind of evidence that the addict's loved ones try desperately to destroy (pouring the gin in the sink, for example), mistakenly focusing on the drug. These caring people naturally focus on the concrete thing, rather than on the disease. So they flush the pills down the toilet and get angry when the addict keeps right on acting like a crazy addict. Robert Lincoln admittedly tried to eradicate any evidence of his mother's impaired mental state, although he never specified what caused this impairment.

In spite of Robert's good intentions, however, we do have some information about Mary Todd Lincoln's use of chemicals. We know that the Lincoln family ordered a great deal of brandy from the drugstore in Springfield. We know that Mary ordered champagne on more than one occasion. We can assume that her doctors gave her opiates for the considerable pain she suffered. We know that she took chloral to help her sleep and that she ordered laudanum before she went to the insane asylum. And we know that in the records of her stay at the asylum there is a conspicuous absence of reference to any drugs that Mary Todd Lincoln was given.

Let us look first at alcohol. Mary Todd Lincoln grew up in the "hard drinking society" of upper class Lexington, Kentucky (Baker 65). Her father's store, one of his many business ventures, sold brandy which he personally purchased in New Orleans and transported to Kentucky. No doubt the Todd men drank, as most men there drank, but Mary probably did not know of her brother Levi's alcoholism until after she had moved away from Lexington (his health declined rapidly after their father's death). No doubt the Todd women drank very little, at least in public.

It has been assumed that because Abraham Lincoln did not drink alcohol, his wife did not drink it either. Indeed, Abraham spoke eloquently in favor of temperance as early as 1842, when he said that drunkenness, which often afflicts the most able among us, "is one of the greatest, if not the very greatest, of all evils among mankind" (Nickolay 9, 105). When he made this statement, he was well aware of other existing evils: women could not vote, our government was exterminating Indian peoples, and slavery was legal in much of the United States. By all accounts Abraham Lincoln avoided this greatest of evils in his personal life by not drinking alcohol. He apparently did not drink it socially and did not need it medicinally. For, as he lamented, in that same temperance speech, doctors at that time routinely prescribed alcohol as effective medication for a host of physical disorders.

At any rate, someone in the Lincoln family in the 1850s used a great deal of brandy for something. According to the records from a Springfield drug store, for example, the Lincoln family purchased within one ten-day period in August, 1853, three pints of brandy. Another such period was June, 1859, when 88% of their bill at the drug store was for two bottles of brandy. This was a low period in Mary Todd Lincoln's life, for Lincoln had just lost his second important political race, her son Robert was about to leave for college in the East, and she had already exhibited her extravagant shopping pattern. We cannot know whether she herself drank that brandy, some of which could also have been used for entertaining, of course, but we can safely assume that if she did drink it, prescribed by her doctor for her nervousness and headache, she would have considered it a medicine. She would have wanted no one to think of her as a "drinker."

In addition to brandy, the Corneau & Diller Drug Store records show that the Lincoln family purchased many other items which also contained alcohol: rum, plain alcohol, pain extractor, wine ipecac, cologne, and various cough syrups, restoratives, cordials, carminatives, balsams, and extracts (Hickey 64-66). Also, in October, 1851, the Lincolns purchased some Spirits Hartshorn, an oily concoction made from roasted bones and added to alcoholic drinks to prevent excessive drinking. This addition made the alcohol unpalatable enough to discourage most people from drinking more than a few sips of it.

In the fall of that same year, Mary Todd Lincoln accompanied her husband to Cincinnati. The hotel where they stayed later sent them a bill for $52 for "several bottles of whisky and brandy and a box of cigars" used for "refreshments for the local Republican committee as well as the entertainment of Mr. and Mrs. Lincoln" (Townsend 282).

During the spring of 1860, when important men from Washington came to Springfield to inform Abraham of his nomination for President, Mary entertained them. Strongly against a "dry" party, she provided brandy and champagne for the guests. Some of these guests pointed out that "Mary Todd Lincoln had violated custom by including alcohol" (Baker 114). Apparently a number of the visitors from the East were temperance men. Mary stood her ground and did not remove the alcohol until finally Abraham intervened.

It has been commonly believed that the Lincolns did not serve alcohol in the White House, but apparently they did. The Turners found three telegrams sent by Mary Todd Lincoln to a wine merchant in New York City. The first, she sent in February, 1862, ordering wine. (This was just before

Willie's death.) The second telegram she sent February 25, 1864, ordering champagne:

> Please send immediately 1 basket champagne, the "Widow Cliquot" brand, [this was crossed out] the other basket of any choice quality you consider desirable].
>
> Mrs Lincoln—
> (Turner 169)

And the third telegram she sent the following day, February 26, 1864, repeating (why?) and doubling her previous order:

> A telegram was sent you in reference to a basket of champagne—Please send a basket of the kind requested also another one, of the choicest quality, you have in store
>
> Mrs Lincoln—
> (Turner 170)

Although we cannot tell whether or not Mary Todd Lincoln herself drank any of this champagne, we can conclude that alcohol was important to her. Alcohol was so important to her that she had to order it sent from New York City! It was so important that she needed it even in the midst of the war. There wasn't enough money to buy boots and blankets for the soldiers, but she bought champagne. It was so important that she did the ordering herself.

In addition to alcohol, we know that Mary Todd Lincoln used opium for her headaches. According to an African American woman, Mariah Vance, who worked for the Lincolns in Springfield, Mary Todd Lincoln drank paregoric frequently and it often caused her to be sick or difficult. One day after Mariah urged Mary to stop drinking this poison, paregoric, Mary answered that:

> if paregoric were poison, the Todd family would have been dead years ago. Some never born. We were raised on it. (Ostendorf and Oleksy, 100)

According to Vance, on numerous occasions she pleaded with Mary Todd Lincoln to stop drinking paregoric and "get some sense into her head."

A member of her family, probably a granddaughter of Mary's sister Elizabeth, confirmed her famous aunt's use of opium:

> Mary Edwards Brown told LIFE magazine in 1959 that her great-aunt, Mrs. Lincoln, had frequent sick headaches which she treated with opium. (Mrs. Lincoln's Obsessions 22)

Which form of opium is not specified, but most likely Mary soon switched from paregoric to a more powerful opiate, laudanum. Most likely she was given laudanum for her headaches, her nervousness and for the deliveries of her babies (her last birth was especially difficult). Such use of laudanum to relieve pain would have been standard medical procedure.

During Mary Todd Lincoln's insanity trial, her chamber maid testified that she had given Mrs. Lincoln laudanum drops when "things became unmanageable" (Ross 310). And two other witnesses testified that they had seen Mary Todd Lincoln take medication. Mrs. Allen, a housekeeper at the Grand Pacific Hotel where Mary Todd Lincoln had been living, said that Mrs. Lincoln had mixed several kinds of medicine together (Chicago *Interocean*, May 20, 1875). Also, a Mrs. Harrington testified that Mrs. Lincoln was "nervous and excitable," and that she "mixed medicines from several bottles that the doctor had left her and took the mixture all at once" (Neely 16).

Furthermore, we know that after her insanity trial, Mary Todd Lincoln visited three different pharmacies in an urgent quest for laudanum. We know that when she finally thought she had it, she drank it right there on the street and then went back inside to order more. She was definitely familiar with this opiate.

The records of one Springfield drugstore show that the Lincolns frequently purchased other forms of opium, such as paregoric and elixir of opium, in addition to the cough syrups and other special mixtures which also contained some opiates. They also purchased, at least once, cocaine.

Any drugs which the Lincolns needed or wanted, however, would have been very easy for them to get. The Lincolns had an account with the Corneau & Diller Drug Store in Springfield, and Mr. Corneau lived right next door to the Lincolns. Furthermore, Mary Todd Lincoln's brother-in-law (husband of Frances) William Wallace and her cousin John Todd were physicians in town. Then later, in Washington, Mary Todd Lincoln had an intricate purchasing network for whatever things she needed, quite possibly including drugs. She also had there at least one physician (Anson Henry) who was a family friend.

In his mother's letters that Robert left for us, there is a conspicuous absence of information concerning exactly what medicine she took for all the pain she had suffered for so many years. We know that she traveled widely from health spa to health spa, that she relied on many different doctors during the last part of her life. We know that she was frequently in pain, yet there is no mention of any specific remedy. It is almost as if someone deliberately wanted there to be no record of any medicine Mary Todd Lincoln took.

One letter remains, dated May, 1870, written from Germany, in which she mentions seeing her doctor in Frankfurt about a new medicine he had given her (Turner 560). There is the previously mentioned and recently found letter to Dr. Danforth in 1874, requesting more chloral. And in 1882, she wrote from New York asking her nephew to "supervise" a small package of medicine she was sending to Springfield (Turner 716). But in all those years of suffering, of consulting different doctors, of visiting different treatment centers, there is almost no specific mention in her hand of the drugs she tried.

We do have references to medicines in Mary's older sister Elizabeth's letters, however, sometime between 1876 and 1880:

> My Dear Mary,
>
> I have just received your letter of the 13th and it truly fills my heart with sorrow to learn of your painful condition—surely you apply to a physician—and why can he not brace you up? I am so anxious about you—If I only had you with me I think you would very soon gain your strength by using some tonics, of a stimulating nature. It is terrible to toss upon a bed unable to sleep. An anodyne should be given you to procure that blessed rest.

Such talk would be natural between sisters when one of them was having health problems—talk of stimulating tonics and anodynes (pain relievers). And then, Elizabeth went on to tell Mary about her own recovery, thanks to her doctor's giving her opium by injection rather than by mouth. She wrote to Mary:

> Dr. Back found that I could not take a sufficient amount of opium to allay pain, without affecting me unpleasantly—

> and had it given as an injection. The result was, comfortable rest, at night. (Insanity File, Baker 342)

In a time when opium was the wonder drug of all time, it is remarkable that this one instance is the only surviving mention of it in all the Mary Todd Lincoln correspondence.

We also know that Mary Todd Lincoln had access, in the early 1870s, to the new drug, chloral hydrate. She herself explained her temporary insanity as the result of her using this new drug (Neely 141). A sedative-hypnotic, like alcohol, chloral made many people, but not all, feel relaxed and sleepy. By 1875, Mary Todd Lincoln "used chloral very freely for the purpose of inducing sleep," according to her sister Elizabeth (Neely 33). Elizabeth would not have felt guilty writing this down, for the medical profession did not yet realize that this drug was also addictive to certain people, and so no stigma was associated with its use. We now know, of course, that chloral is a mood-changing chemical very similar to alcohol and barbiturates and that it would indeed feed a chemical addiction:

> Because all sedative-hypnotics are similar, they are cross-tolerant. This means that as an individual is developing tolerance for alcohol, let's say, he or she is also developing tolerance for barbiturates, benzodiazepines and all other drugs in this group, whether he or she has taken them or not. (Seymore 42)

In other words, Mary Todd Lincoln had already developed a tolerance for alcohol, although she may not have realized this, and she was probably still using it, at least in the form of laudanum, when she began taking chloral.

Indeed, chloral was far from the "harmless drug," which Neely termed it after checking three articles in the *American*

Journal of Insanity (none written later than 1878). Initially, the drug was welcomed in the 1870s, as a way to quiet people who needed quieting. Mental patients, for example, were often given choral at night to make them sleep. It was also prescribed for headache (Crothers 289). An English physician, a chloral addict himself since 1871, wrote:

> But little was then known of the after effects of chloral even by medical men. It was a new medicine, and worked wonders—they lauded it to the skies. (Stables 181)

The sad result, however, was a "new class of drunkards" in England.

In America also many people became addicted to chloral (Morgan 109). In 1881, Kane wrote that there were many chloral addicts, most of them in the educated classes, and most of them with a tendency to insanity, alcoholism, or opiate addiction in their families (Kane 162). He found that many of these addicts used chloral as a substitute for alcohol, and that many of them later switched to opiates. Other doctors, such as Crothers in 1902, reported that chloral caused delusions and hallucinations (Crothers 288), and in some people "general derangement" (Crothers 289) or even insanity (Hubbard 204, Kane 172).

As better barbiturate-type drugs were invented (such as Valium), drugs that did not taste bad and irritate the stomach as chloral did, chloral use diminished considerably. It is still available today by prescription, however, and in the current drug reference books the mention of chloral hydrate is always accompanied by a strong warning not to use it with alcohol.

The one period in Mary Todd Lincoln's life when we might expect to have some accurate information about what medication she was taking was during her stay at Bellevue

Place, the insane asylum in Batavia, Illinois. She spent almost four months there, from May 20 to September 11, 1875. The asylum kept anecdotal records, handwritten, on each patient.

According to these records, covering the period 1873 through 1875, all the patients were women, and almost all of them were given mood-changing drugs, particularly chloral, alcohol (in the form of beer, ale, or whiskey), and morphine (morphia). Also frequently mentioned were potassium bromide, cannabis, quinine, and conium (Batavia patient records). For example, Jenny McDonald woke up at 3 o'clock every morning and made a lot of noise; she was given chloral so she would sleep until morning. Theresa McGuire was feeble, emaciated—"fatal exhaustion seems probable." She was given egg nog, morphia, and quinine three times a day, even though she objected to taking any medicine. In June, Mary Wheaton was on chloral and conium, by August she was having night sweats and was given beer and later ale. Mrs. Hall and Minnie Judd were routinely given chloral at night. Mrs. Hatch and Mrs. Terry were given hypodermic injections of morphia during the day and chloral at bedtime. Mrs. Munger went into the water closet and stabbed herself in the abdomen with a large carving knife; she was put on opiates. Mrs. Harcourt was weak and would not eat; she was given egg nog with whiskey—a large goblet full three times a day—and chloral at night, but one night the chloral did not do its job and she needed more twice during the night because she was excited and noisy. In the morning she died: "The case terminated with unexpected suddenness" (September 23, 1874). It would appear, then, that mood-changing chemicals were routinely given to Bellevue patients.

But not to Mary Todd Lincoln? These patient records contain no mention of any medications given to Mrs.

Lincoln. Given the context, the informative notations on other patients, this absence of information is conspicuous indeed. Furthermore, Mary Todd Lincoln's records covering the four months that she was there are written in what appears to be the same hand, in what appears to be a vague and hasty manner. Possibly someone gave instructions to write no specific details of Mary Todd Lincoln's treatment there, or possibly someone later altered that portion of the Bellevue records in order to obfuscate the medication issue. In fact, it seems highly likely that Mary Todd Lincoln's asylum records were tampered with by some well-meaning person in order to protect her privacy and protect the asylum.

The result is that the notations mentioning Mary Todd Lincoln were in stark contrast to the notations for most of the other patients. Usually the notation about her was very brief, describing only her general manner that day: "Lies in bed much of the time," or "Does not talk much to anyone," or "had a fit of crying today," but most entries just described her "as usual today." For us there is very little information in these entries, and we cannot help wondering why the nurses mentioned the medications the other women were getting, but nothing about what Mary Todd Lincoln surely received. Could it really be that in such a place at such a time Mary Todd Lincoln was receiving no chemicals? Surely not. The fact that many Bellevue patients received morphine (morphia), that Mary Todd Lincoln slept a lot, was noticeably calm most of the time, and was often sensitive to the noise of the carpenters (July 7, 1875), would indicate that she might well have been taking morphine also.

In summary, then, throughout her adult life, Mary Todd Lincoln did have access to a number of mood-changing chemicals. She purchased brandy and champagne, but also a variety of other items containing alcohol. She frequently used paregoric, and she was almost surely given laudanum for her headaches and other pains, such as childbirth. During the period before her trial, she is known to have used chloral hydrate, and witnesses at the trial reported that she mixed various medicines given her by her doctor. Mary Todd Lincoln clearly had access to alcohol, laudanum, and chloral, and most likely she was also given morphine, as were many of the other patients at Bellevue.

In What Ways Did She Behave Like an Addict?

> Very few people live part of their life as good, intelligent, sane people and then start acting bad, stupid, and/or crazy unless alcohol and drugs are the culprit. (O'Neill 6)

That is exactly what Mary Todd Lincoln did. She lived the first part of her life as a good, intelligent, sane woman, and then she started acting bad, stupid, and crazy. Her addiction was the culprit.

In the language of the chemical dependency field, we can say that her unique Mary Todd Lincoln personality deteriorated and that increasingly, inadvertently, she assumed the classic personality of the addict. This personality profile, as outlined in the Appendix, consists of five types of erratic behavior: acting afraid, angry, withdrawn, desperate, and physically sick. The cluster of these behaviors, the negative pattern they create, is the glaring sign of chemical addiction. All addicts exhibit this pattern. Let us look again at Mary Todd Lincoln in terms of each of these addict behaviors.

Fearful. On a scale from nervousness (a word that Mary Todd Lincoln used a lot about herself) to paranoia, Mary Todd Lincoln veered increasingly toward the latter. By 1867, when she wrote this to Elizabeth Keckley, it was a fairly typical remark from Mary, who clearly did not want to be as nervous as she increasingly was: "Forget my fright and nervousness of the evening before" (Keckley 301). And later that same year:

> Never, dear Lizzie, think of my great nervousness the night before we parted; I had been so harassed with my fears. (Keckley 362)

Often her nervousness interfered very much with her life, and often she apologized for it, as she wrote in 1869:

> Between indisposition, sad, & anxious THOUGHTS & every thing else—I have grown very nervous, & can now scarcely read & certainly cannot do any thing useful. (Turner 525)

Another example of her nervousness was her extreme sensitivity (probably a result of the opiates in her system) to noise on at least two documented occasions. The first was just after her husband's death when carpenters were constructing a wooden platform in some part of the White House. The son of a friend of Mary Todd Lincoln's kindly asked the carpenters not to take the wooden boards down (after the funeral ceremonies) because:

> Mrs. Lincoln is very much disturbed by noise. The other night when putting them up, every plank that dropped gave her a spasm and every nail that was driven seemed to her like a pistol shot. (Randall 385)

The second instance of Mary Todd Lincoln's complaining about loud noises was July 7, 1875, at Bellevue Insane Asylum, when again the noise of carpenters irritated her.

Toward the end of her White House years, however, and during the ensuing period before her insanity trial, Mary Todd Lincoln was often more than nervous. She was so afraid that she sometimes sounded quite paranoid. As Keckley said:

> She seemed to read impending danger in every rustling leaf, in every whisper of the wind. (Keckley 120)

She saw danger in attending her son Robert's wedding. Mary wrote that she wanted to see it, but "The terror of having to proceed to Washington to witness it, almost overpowers me" (Sandburg 285). A few years later Robert hired a nurse, Mrs. Fitzgerald, to accompany his mother on her unpredictable wanderings around the country. Mrs. Fitzgerald later wrote that Mary Todd Lincoln clearly lived in a state of "mortal fear" of such terrible things as the walls of the room falling down upon her or of the city around her catching fire (Ross 306).

Randall, a most sympathetic and thorough biographer, described how persecuted Mary Todd Lincoln felt during the spring of 1875:

> her life had become a nightmare of fear. She walked the floor through sleepless nights, keeping the gas turned high against the threat of the dark, eyeing her windows with dread of the nameless terror that might enter through them. . . Her personal pride was drowned in fear. (Randall 429)

One of the reasons Mary returned to Chicago (from wandering in Florida) that spring was that she was certain that Robert was in some terrible danger. She sent him a frantic telegram urging him to stay alive for her sake. He met her at the train and assured her that he was just fine, and then he took an adjacent room in her hotel so that he could watch over her. One night he found her, half-dressed, in an elevator headed down to the hotel lobby. When he tried to guide her back to her room, she resisted and accused him of trying to murder her (Ross 309).

At her insanity trial, a hotel housekeeper testified that Mary Todd Lincoln was terrified of being alone, a waiter testified that Mary Todd Lincoln had one time appeared confused, saying over and over again that she was afraid (Baker 320), and a doctor testified that Mrs. Lincoln had imagined that she was poisoned by a stranger on the train on her way home from Florida (Neely 14). After the trial it was apparent that Mary Todd Lincoln trusted nobody, for she was found to have all her money, $56,000 in securities, sewn into her skirt.

So, yes, like the typical active chemical addict, Mary Todd Lincoln was increasingly very afraid of all kinds of things, real and imagined, but mostly imagined. She was afraid of being alone, afraid another woman would take Abraham away from her, afraid that her loved ones were in constant danger, afraid of fire sometimes, afraid of threatening strangers in the dark, even afraid, when her mind was most disoriented, that her own son was trying to murder her. The fact that we look back and say that she imagined these things she feared, however, does in no way diminish the genuine fear that she felt. She was, much of the time, afraid.

Angry. Like other active chemical addicts, Mary Todd Lincoln was prone to "unreasonable outbursts of anger"

(Evans 70). The emphasis is on the word "unreasonable," for her sudden rages of temper, such as the unfortunate time at City Point, usually seemed unwarranted. After such outbursts, however, she was full of regret:

> Her volatile temper outbursts would be followed by apologies and promises but often after the harm had been done. (Suarez 817)

This was her pattern, a cycle of angry outbursts, regret, the accumulating of more resentment, the nurturing of more grudges, and then an outburst again. It almost seemed that her anger was lurking there under the surface, just waiting for the merest excuse to erupt.

After the insanity trial, her anger often focused on Robert. While Mary was visiting her sister and brother-in-law, Robert's aunt and uncle, in Springfield, on a kind of "home pass" from Bellevue, Robert's uncle wrote to him:

> I am sorry to say that your mother has for the last month been very much embittered against you and has on several occasions said that she had hired two men to take your life. (Neely 92)

Although this threat was no doubt an empty one, it is nevertheless another example of Mary Todd Lincoln's unreasonable anger.

She frequently directed her anger at certain individuals who happened also to be fellow addicts. Baker suggested that Mary Todd Lincoln was angry with her daughter-in-law because she knew the "dark secret" of Mary Harlan Lincoln's alcoholism (Baker 310). Mary Todd Lincoln also cherished her anger for General Grant, a known alcoholic, dismissing him in a letter (1869) as "that small specimen of humanity"

(Turner 518). She called Andrew Johnson, who gave a drunken speech at Lincoln's second inauguration, "that miserable inebriate Johnson" (Turner 345). And William Herndon, a law partner of Abraham's, made Mary's blood boil; she called him many things: a "dirty dog" (Turner 416), a "hopeless inebriate" (Randall 115), a "wretch" and a "vile, unprincipled and DEBASED character" (Turner 599), a "liar" (Turner 604), and a "wretched drunken madman" (Turner 606).

Mary Todd Lincoln even felt anger toward whole countries of people. She lived among the Germans, sent her son Tad to a German school, and took advantage of their medical advances, yet she seemed to turn against them. They were only, she said, "cold and unsympathizing strangers who never dreamed of my anguish" (Baker 303). Similarly, she changed her mind completely about the French. Mary Todd Lincoln had been educated in a French school, spoke fluent French, and liked to read French literature. She chose at one point to live in France, and in 1876, she wrote from France that she had just purchased a five volume history of France, "the latest history of this beautiful land" (Turner 618). Yet later she suddenly decided that the French people were "the most unprincipled, heartless, avaricious people on the face of the earth. With the exception of a VERY FEW, I detest them all" (Turner 699).

Mary Todd Lincoln increasingly behaved like an angry woman. Unreasonable anger is one of the trademarks of the active chemical addict, and it became one of her trademarks as well.

Withdrawn. Just as fear breeds anger, anger can foster loneliness. Typically, the addict is unpredictably angry with the people around her, hurts them, regrets this, and gradually pulls away from them. Mary Todd Lincoln definitely exhibited this pattern. But there is another force that compels the addict to withdraw and that is her preoccupation with herself and her chief focus, getting her drug. This deepening self-centeredness takes two forms: self pity and secretiveness. Because in order to survive, the addict must spend increasing amounts of energy on herself, she has very little left for other people.

Mary Todd Lincoln, as her addiction deepened, quite rightly felt very sorry for herself. We notice this first when she was still in the White House. After Willie's death in 1862, Mary Todd Lincoln was incapacitated for three months:

> more alone, frightened, and despairing than ever before. For three months following the funeral, she lay lost in the most abject misery, wild grief alternating with periods of paralyzing depression. She was unable to function, or to write to her family or friends. (Turner 121)

No doubt Mary Todd Lincoln was given opiates then, to calm her.

In 1867, the year of the infamous Old Clothes Sale, Mrs. Lincoln wrote to Elizabeth Keckley:

> I am friendless... What a world of anguish this is and how I have been made to suffer. (Turner 441)

Here she was referring to her financial situation. She felt that Congress had treated her unfairly, not providing her with enough income to live as she needed to live. In that same year she wrote to Elizabeth Keckley concerning Frederick Douglass's impending visit to Chicago:

> Tell him, for me, he must call and see me; give him my number. If I had been able to retain a house, I should have offered him apartments when he came to C.; as it is, I have to content MYSELF with lodgings. An ungrateful country this! (Keckley 361)

It bothered her that she lived in reduced circumstances:

> I have been compelled from a pitiful income to make a boarding-house of my home, as I now am doing, think you that it does not rankle in my heart? Fortunately, with my husband's great, great love for me—the knowledge of this future for his petted and idolized wife was spared him. (Keckley 352)

> The "petty sum" that Congress allowed her was a "meagreness," she whined, given grudgingly by rich men who now "traduced and vilified the loved wife of the great man who made them." (Keckley 352)

Because she felt so poor (even though she was not), she wrote in 1870 from Germany that she had no one to care for her when she was sick:

> I passed a sleepless, miserable night & must remain very quiet to day—as I have a fever upon me—with great & burning pain in my spine—with no one near me to hand me a glass of water if I was dying. (Sandburg 291)

During that same year she wrote:

> You can imagine or rather you CANNOT—but I have lived through THIS RECENT time, with only a GRIM faced landlady, to look in upon me, once in a few hours. (Turner 546)

Yet this letter, also written in 1870 from Germany, is the epitome of Mary Todd Lincoln's self pity:

> All my sorrow—my uncomfortable surroundings—have brought me very near the brink of the grave, and there are moments of each day , when I feel the greatest repugnance—to return to the FEARFUL BATTLE OF LIFE—which has broken my heart. I must accept my terrible fate—to undergo DAILY CRUCIFIXION—knowing that in GOD'S OWN TIME—the weary & heavy laden—will be loosed from the bonds of earth. (Turner 553)

Of course she must have been feeling very bad—lonely, depressed, and in pain. But daily crucifixion! She had become very self-centered indeed.

The other aspect of an addict's self-centeredness is secretiveness. The addict *must* (it is not a question of wanting) secure her supply. Especially during the last third of her life, Mary Todd Lincoln was very secretive, particularly about money. To maintain her addiction, she would have needed contacts, access to money, people to shop for her, excuses to shop herself, places to hide medicine, people to destroy pharmacy records, and much more. As we can see from the following examples, she sometimes went to elaborate lengths to guard her secrets.

One such secret surfaced in 1861, concerning Mary's relationship with William Wood, Commissioner of Public Buildings, who accompanied her on shopping expeditions to New York and helped her juggle accounts so that at least some of her bills got paid. Apparently there was a near scandal about all this and the Lincolns even had a major fight over it. People have assumed that scandal implied romance, but it could rather have implied (the information coming from an anonymous letter) purchasing alcohol or opiates (medicines) surreptitiously so that no one in the family would know how much was really being purchased. At any rate, Mary Todd Lincoln was forced to edge away from Wood.

Then there was the storm of protest in January, 1865, over Mary Todd Lincoln's peremptory firing of the White House doorman, who had ruled at his post for a long time. His name was "Old Edward" McManus, and he had been quite a character, well known and respected, but nobody seemed willing to say why Mrs. Lincoln abruptly dismissed him. The Turners speculated: "Apparently Edward could not be trusted with Mrs. Lincoln's secrets, which were many" (Turner 197). And Edward McManus would have known how often the delivery boy from the pharmacy came to the White House, what he delivered, and for whom.

During the years after Tad's death, clearly one of the bleakest periods in Mary Todd Lincoln's life, she had many secrets. Because Robert often did not even know which state she was in, he hired a nurse to accompany her part of the time. Then when she returned to Chicago in 1875, he hired Pinkerton detectives to follow her around town. We don't know what they found, but we do know that she did a lot of shopping, literally every day, and that she had many unopened packages in her hotel room closet. When she suddenly had to leave for Bellevue, she had many footstools that she emphatically wanted to take along.

While Mary Todd Lincoln was at Bellevue, she was still permitted to go shopping in the town (escorted, of course), and she still stored packages in her trunks. Robert visited her there and later wrote his aunt about his mother: "she usually appeared to me personally to be perfectly calm & sane when I saw her in the evening, except that she consistently denied (usually) having been out of her room"

(Neely 97). So Mary Todd Lincoln even had secrets in the insane asylum.

When Mary left Bellevue for a temporary stay in Springfield with her sister Elizabeth Edwards, Mr. Edwards wrote that they had no idea what Mary did with the income Robert sent her each month (Neely 83). Furthermore, he said that Mary did her buying (which took half of each day) and hoarding in secret, having the things she purchased sent directly to her rooms (Neely 95). Elizabeth agreed that Mary was "very secretive" about her purchases and that the merchants (in a relatively small city where the Edwardses were a very prominent family) did not reveal to her Mary's secrets.

During Mary's second and last stay in Europe, she frequently mentioned in her letters that she had always bypassed Customs when returning to America and she certainly did not want this privilege to change. It seemed important to her that she not have her trunks examined. Perhaps she did not want to pay duty, as has been previously assumed, or perhaps in her trunks she had medicines which she wanted to conceal. She wrote from Europe to her nephew in 1880:

> You wrote me that your kind, good Grandfather had letters that would pass me through the Custom House, I entreat you with HIS invaluable influence, to secure me FREE transport, for my baggage, which HAS ALWAYS been accorded me in Europe without a QUESTION or a trunk being opened. (Turner 700)

This "kind, good Grandfather" was her brother-in-law, Ninian Edwards, Elizabeth's husband. Mary had stayed in his house for long periods of time and he had been instrumental in getting her legally restored to sanity, so why did she not write to him herself? It was clearly very important to her to avoid customs—so important that she would use all the leverage she had—yet there was apparently something she was hiding from him.

Then, of course, when Mary Todd Lincoln returned to this country, her remaining time in her sister's house in Springfield was pretty much shrouded in mystery. We know that she kept to herself in a darkened room and that people who knew she was there thought she was very strange. By the end, then, her whole life seemed to be a secret, and even, until now, the cause of her death was a secret too.

Sometimes because of anger, but also because of her growing self-centeredness, Mary Todd Lincoln increasingly withdrew from her family and friends. After Willie's death, she withdrew even from her son Tad, who was only nine, who was ill, and who was also grieving for his dead brother. Her sister Elizabeth, who was (at Abraham's request) staying with Mary during these months, wrote sadly of Tad's mother: "His mother has been but little with him, being utterly unable to control her feelings" (Randall 287).

Although Mary Todd Lincoln was a gracious hostess at the White House, she did not make close friends in Washington. And she made no effort to be civil even to someone like Julia Grant, whom Mary probably would have been drawn to during an earlier time in her life. During this same period also, Mary lost touch with her favorite cousin, Emilie Helm. Politics were involved here too, but nevertheless, it was one more special person in Mary Todd Lincoln's life whom she pulled away from.

After Lincoln's assassination, Mary withdrew even more: "She was becoming more of a stranger, an alien to some who had known her for years" (Sandburg 133). Mary did not seem to listen to her sisters who urged her to face her loss and get on with her life in a sensible, practical way:

> Her sisters and other relatives who voiced to Mary their indignant protests, entreating her to curb her excitement and eccentricity, only incurred her anger and had become estranged from her. (Helm 266)

Among the Todds, at this point, Mary seems to have been on good terms only with her sister Elizabeth, and she soon became estranged even from her—until Mary, at Bellevue, needed a refuge to come to and Elizabeth provided it.

During this same difficult time in her life, Mary, in a long letter to Elizabeth Keckley (about her only real friend now), told the strange but touching story of her surprise encounter on a train with the elegant Mr. S. whom she had clearly known well and liked in her Washington days. People have assumed that this Mr. S. was her friend Charles Sumner. Oddly, seeing him through her veil very much disconcerted her, and she physically withdrew, making up a story about needing to go get a cup of tea for her lady friend who had a headache. Apparently then *he* went to get a cup of tea for her and brought it back himself:

> I was a good deal annoyed by seeing him, and he was so agitated that he spilled half of the cup over my ELEGANTLY GLOVED hands. HE looked very sad. . . Pity for me, I fear, has something to do with all this. I never saw his manner SO gentle and sad. (Keckley 300)

Every addict who has withdrawn and acted strangely has seen that look in a friend's eyes. After Mr. S. left the room, Mary threw the tea he had given her out the window and shed "bitter tears."

Mary Todd Lincoln had withdrawn from her family, though not yet from Robert and his wife, but soon she also withdrew from her good friend, Elizabeth Keckley. A former slave, Elizabeth had become a sought-after seamstress in Washington, where she sewed for Mary Todd Lincoln and other prominent ladies. After Mary left Washington, she continued to depend on Elizabeth, to confide in her by letter, to ask her for help. It was Elizabeth whom Mary turned to when she, in Chicago, wanted to sell her old clothes in New York, and it was Elizabeth who left her work in Washington to go to New York and make the arrangements. Mary Todd Lincoln appreciated this help and repeatedly pledged her friendship: "I feel as if I had not a friend in the world save yourself" (Keckley 347). She also promised Elizabeth monetary payment, for she knew Elizabeth worked hard for a meager living, but Mary never did pay her. When Mary Todd Lincoln heard about the book that Elizabeth later published, a small book which included a defense of the Old Clothes Sale and some letters from Mrs. Lincoln, she withdrew completely from Elizabeth Keckley. Mary Todd Lincoln turned her back on what had been a vital friendship.

After Tad's death in 1871, Mary Todd Lincoln withdrew completely. We have very few of her letters from this period, probably because she was so withdrawn:

> In the years following Tad's death, Mrs. Lincoln all but disappeared from sight. Her son's illness and the shock of his death had taxed her physically almost beyond endurance; mentally, she was in a state of deep despondency. She was interested in very little and scarcely stayed in one place long enough to maintain a correspondence with anyone. (Turner 595)

Then there was Mary Todd Lincoln's insanity trial. The only Lincoln or Todd present was Mary Todd Lincoln's son

Robert, who testified against her (or *for* her, depending on your point of view). She felt that she had no friends in that courtroom, and we have to admit that, with the exception of Robert, she probably did not have any. Mary was alone.

That Mary Todd Lincoln was a devoted, caring mother, we know, but she did not attend any of the funerals held for her three sons or her husband. At each funeral, of course, there were other family members, also grieving, but Mary Todd Lincoln, unable to consider their grief, withdrew into herself. Like the active chemical addict, she continued to become more and more withdrawn and depressed.

Desperate. As the addict senses that she is losing her inner battle of control, she becomes increasingly desperate. Ever more frantically she seeks to control something that she can control, something concrete. She temporarily reassures herself that this different spouse or different house will make things better. That buying more of this or that will make her feel secure. That if she can just, with all the effort she can muster, look normal, everything will be okay. Or that, if all else fails, she can just die and escape once and for all. The doomed addict desperately wants to regain control of her life even if it means deciding to end it.

Mary Todd Lincoln grew increasingly desperate in her later years. We can see five ways in which she sought to regain some control over her life. 1) She moved around a lot (called "geographical cure" in addiction terminology). 2) She had spurts of grandiosity. 3) She protected her supply. 4) She tried so hard to appear "normal" that she appeared to ricochet back and forth into insanity. 5) She frequently became so desperate that she wished to die.

She moved around frequently after her husband was killed. She naturally wanted to leave Washington then, but she did not go back to Lexington, where she had family, or to

Springfield, where she had most recently and most happily lived. She had many relatives in Springfield, and she still owned a house there. Instead, she went to Chicago, but moved around even in that city. Some places she sought out for her health, but most of the time she seemed to be wandering rather aimlessly.

Tad went along, of course. Because of their moving, he went to four different schools in the first two years after his father's murder. He was twelve when his father died, and in Tad's remaining six years of life he was never in the same school for more than one year.

Mary Todd Lincoln's wandering in this country after the assassination and her wandering in Europe before 1871, however, were nothing compared to her restlessness here after Tad died. It was this restlessness, in part, that worried Robert Lincoln, for he often did not know where his mother was. Then after Mary Todd Lincoln was released from Bellevue and declared sane again, she soon resumed her wanderings in Europe. This time, with no son to be responsible for, she moved around erratically. And even in her final year of life, back in Springfield, she made a trip to New York City (for health reasons, but nevertheless a long journey).

Mary Todd Lincoln also had spurts of grandiosity, a tendency that many active addicts have. Typically this grandiosity shows up as a secondary addiction, such as gambling or sex or shopping. Sometimes it merely shows up in the odd remark or one obsessive habit. It is very common, however.

Mary Todd Lincoln's compulsive shopping was an example of grandiosity. It was a desperate attempt to establish a kind of control over something outside herself. Similarly, the Old Clothes Sale was a grandiose scheme, poorly conceived, poorly executed. The original Mary Todd

Lincoln would never have nurtured such a scheme—she wouldn't have been so deluded about the money, and she wouldn't have wanted to take the risk, and she would have been much too smart, in her right mind, to be fooled in the deal.

Elizabeth Keckley mentioned an interesting detail of Mary Todd Lincoln's deal to sell her old clothes. The grandiosity is evident. Mary wrote from Chicago to Elizabeth in Washington asking her to make hotel reservations in New York for her, under the name of Mrs. Clarke. This was a bizarre request and impossible for Elizabeth to carry out. By the time Elizabeth reached New York, Mary was already there, registered as Mrs. Clarke. When Mary asked them to give Elizabeth a room next to hers, they rudely refused. Finally they relented and gave Elizabeth a room on the fifth floor. Mary moved up there too in protest, except the protest was pointless because the hotel people did not know who she really was. Then when Elizabeth went down to have some supper, they refused to serve her. Mary Todd Lincoln wanted to take Elizabeth out in the street in search of some supper, but Elizabeth, not wanting Mrs. Lincoln to take this risk, went to bed without supper. This entire charade was grandiose on the part of Mary Todd Lincoln, at the expense of Elizabeth, who closed her shop in Washington to come to New York on this humiliating wild goose chase.

The clearest example that Mary Todd Lincoln had the addict's instinct to protect her supply was her infamous "suicide attempt" after her insanity trial. We remember that Mary Todd Lincoln was surprised that afternoon by the man who escorted her to the trial, so she had not expected to spend her day that way. (An addict needs to plan carefully, always, so as never to run out.) She insisted that before she go along with him, she be permitted to change her dress. He was reluctant to permit this, for there was no woman present to keep an eye on Mrs. Lincoln, but he finally relented. Thus, Mary was alone in her closet for a short while. She could have taken her laudanum then.

The trial lasted several hours, after which she returned to her hotel, where two guards were to watch her. She eluded both of them, however, for she was desperate to get some more laudanum. So desperate that when the first druggist refused her (Why? Because he knew her habit.), she went (a proper lady did not go running around the streets like that) to a second and then to a third druggist. When she finally had a vial of what she thought was laudanum, she gulped the whole thing down right there in the street and went back into the pharmacy to buy some more. Not because she wanted to kill herself, but because she desperately needed her drug. Hirschhorn, a physician, says that during this famous episode, Mary Todd Lincoln was requesting a dangerous amount of laudanum, "*unless* she was addicted to laudanum," in which case she would be used to that much and even more (Hirschhorn 97). Mary Todd Lincoln needed more.

During this same period, at the hotel in Chicago, before the trial, Robert Lincoln hired two Pinkerton detectives to follow his mother. Most sons do not need to resort to this subterfuge. The detectives then reported to Robert that Mary Todd Lincoln was being visited by "suspicious looking persons" (Friedman 48). The logical explanation would be that Mary Todd Lincoln had dealers there, as she had in the White House, who could procure medications for her in secret.

We can also surmise that the pattern of Mary Todd Lincoln's shopping trips may have been related to her need to protect her supply. In the White House her need for fancy clothes and fancy furnishings may have been in part a cover for her need for her medicine. Just as her many trunks and boxes (or footstools) could have served as a respectable way for a rich lady to hide her medicine when she traveled.

According to a Chicago newspaper, Mrs. Lincoln told Dr. Danforth, a witness at her trial, that on her way back to Chicago from Florida (when she was so frantic about Robert), some strangers put poison in her coffee. She then drank not one, but two cups of the coffee that she believed was poisoned. This sounds like some of her craziness, but the part about quickly downing two cups of drugged coffee sounds very much like something an addict would do. After all, the very word poison acquires a different meaning in the context of an addiction, for the addict's poison is the very thing she must have. And gulping and guzzling are natural behaviors for an active addict.

The fourth kind of desperation we see in Mary Todd Lincoln's behavior was what appeared to be her alternating sanity and insanity. From her late White House days until the end of her life, she seemed to have intervals of what appeared to be insanity. As already described in chapter I, her behavior was often unpredictable, so unpredictable at times that the people around her assumed that only an insane person would behave that way.

Robert said that his mother was insane only about money. Mary Todd Lincoln apparently admitted to her sister Elizabeth that her difficulties that spring of 1875 were caused by her use of chloral hydrate, and Elizabeth agreed with this explanation. Helm concluded that Mary's mental troubles were the result of her overwhelming troubles—headaches, grief, debts, loneliness. Randall pointed to menopause. Evans talked of her inherited personality difficulties, and Turner, of her increasingly erratic behavior, but both found her sane. Neely found her sane except for the unfortunate spring of 1875, and Baker found her sane, but suffering from the fear of being abandoned yet again. All of these people, kind and interested in Mary Todd Lincoln, clearly felt that they had to come up with some explanation: either this woman was technically insane, but sometimes behaved as if she were sane, or she was really quite sane but had lapses of what could appear to be insanity. Even the court said yes and no: insane in 1875, sane in 1876. What can we make of this?

An addict acts that way. She is insane, but then again she is not; sometimes she is weird, sometimes she is just her own sweet self. She can't help this. But she does sense that she is deviating from her normal ways and tries desperately to compensate. She exerts enormous amounts of energy and will into acting and being what the world around her will think is normal. It never works for long, of course, because she is resisting an irresistible force.

Mary Todd Lincoln tried to be normal. She apologized for her outbursts, for her "nervousness." She tried to explain her physical ills, so that at least people would think her more sick than crazy. She sought out new doctors, new medicines, new healing places. For a long time she herself probably did not know what was wrong. But she was never able to convince the people around her that she was all right. They worried and looked for a way to explain her flickers of insanity until by the end of her life they gave up on her, left her alone with whatever it was that plagued her. She too retreated and let the addiction consume her.

The last example of Mary Todd Lincoln's desperation was her talk of death, her own death. If she couldn't control her life, she might as well end it. The addict, swerving in and out of sanity, grows weary and frightened and ready to quit, to escape. Mary Todd Lincoln said to Elizabeth Keckley:

> I should like to live for my sons, but life is so full of misery that I would rather die. (Keckley 200)

And two years later, in 1867, she wrote to Elizabeth Keckley:

> I am so miserable I feel like taking my own life. (Keckley 363)

One year later:

> Troubles and misfortunes are fast overwhelming me; may THE END soon come. (Keckley 368)

And in 1869:

> Death would be far more preferable to me, than my present life. (Turner 524)

It is clear that Mary Todd Lincoln often felt that death would be preferable to life.

Physically ill. Mary Todd Lincoln also behaved like an addict by acting very sick much of the time, increasingly so as she grew older. In addition to the pain she felt, we can see evidence of her body's illness in how she looked, how she felt, and how she acted.

Mary Todd Lincoln looked, in several important ways, like a suffering addict. As we have seen, the Mary Todd Lincoln who lived at the White House took great pride in her elegant appearance. By 1875, however, she had appeared in public carelessly dressed or even unkempt. A Chicago newspaper said of her: "the habit of a lifetime was neglected and she at times failed to give thought to neatness in dress" (*Interocean* May 20, 1875). Such personal neglect is eventually the characteristic of the chemical addict.

Another physical characteristic is sudden and unexplained changes in weight. For example, Mary Todd Lincoln's "puffiness of face" (Evans 340) or her "great bloat," as she herself called it, is a common symptom of alcohol addiction. Similarly, her later rapid loss of weight when she suddenly became "thin, almost wizened" (Evans 279), is symptomatic of all progressing chemical addiction as the addict loses interest in eating.

Perhaps the most indicative aspect of Mary Todd Lincoln's appearance was that she often appeared to be sedated, as indeed she was. Six weeks after Abraham's death, when Robert and the others were finally able to dislodge Mary from the White House, she left for Chicago. Accompanying her on the 54-hour train ride were her two sons, Elizabeth Keckley, Dr. Anson Henry, and William Crook, a White House guard. Crook later wrote of Mary Todd Lincoln that when she was not weeping, she was in a daze, "almost a stupor," and that she hardly spoke (Van der Heuvel 185). And according to Mary Todd Lincoln's friend Rev. Miner, she *was* in a stupor at this time:

> She told me that she had no knowledge of the time when they took her away, nor or anything else for many days after. (Miner)

In addiction terminology, Mary Todd Lincoln was perhaps in a blackout.

Baker describes Mary Todd Lincoln in her last photograph (1873) as having eyes that are "glassy and clouded" (Baker 311). And two years later, at one of the most public times of her life, her insanity trial, Mary Todd Lincoln was strangely calm:

> Her composure was so striking and so much at variance with her excitable nature that some wondered if she had been given a sedative before the ordeal began. (Ross 310)

Of course, after her understandable outrage at being summoned to her own trial, we remember that she convinced her escort to permit her to retire alone for a few minutes to change her dress in her closet where her many packages from her "shopping" were stored. Surely she needed her medicine then.

Throughout the three hours of her trial, Mary Todd Lincoln was, according to all newspaper reports, stolid and unmoved. Shopkeepers and housekeepers described her crazy shopping, her crazy mutterings. She was unmoved. Her only son, with tears in his eyes, testified against her, testified that she was insane and should be locked up in a lunatic asylum. And she was unmoved. Extraordinary behavior for a healthy person, but not for an addict who was numbed to what was happening around her.

Even a few years later when Mary Todd Lincoln was returning from Europe, the actress Sarah Bernhardt, who was on the same boat, described Mary as a sad, confused little woman who spoke in a "gentle, dreamy voice" (Turner 704). By this time Mary Todd Lincoln was in a complete fog most of the time, "little cognizant of what was taking place about her" (Evans 310). And then she died.

In addition to looking like an addict, Mary Todd Lincoln also felt like one. She suffered much pain, as we have seen. Some of this pain, such as her frequent "neuralgic" pain in her back and limbs, was symptomatic of opiate addiction (withdrawal pains). Similarly, her nervousness, chills, coughing, trouble sleeping, loss of appetite, proneness to infections were all common symptoms of chemical addiction. And all of these contributed to her general feeling of being much older than she actually was. She wrote, at age 51, "I sometimes feel as if I had lived a century" (Turner 530). Most active addicts eventually feel this way.

Of particular note are the opiate addiction symptoms that plagued Mary Todd Lincoln toward the end of her life. The opiates slow down the body's liquids, so that normal activities such as tearing, sweating, and elimination come almost to a standstill. As the drug wears off, of course, these liquids begin to gush again. Mary Todd Lincoln's frequent crying jags during stressful periods (Keckley 116, 213) may have been a result of the chemically induced fluid imbalance in her body, as may also have been her occasional dropsical condition (Baker 310), her "continual running waters" (Ross 327), her constant thirst (Evans 342), and her "sore and inflamed eyes" (Turner 467).

Indeed, the opiates do two stressful things to the eye. They temporarily dry up the natural lubricants, resulting in irritation and possible infection (often conjunctivitis, for example). They also cause the pupils of the eyes to constrict, resulting in very limited, often light-sensitive vision. Thus, in 1869, Mary Todd Lincoln could "scarcely read" (Turner 524), later her vision was "VERY obscured" (Turner 711), an ophthalmologist diagnosed her "reflex paralysis of the iris" [constricted pupils] (Baker 368), and she spent her last days in Springfield in a darkened room.

Not only did Mary Todd Lincoln look and feel very much the way an active chemical addict looks and feels, but also she did some things that addicts typically do as they struggle for that inner control, as they vacillate in and out of their craziness. Most obviously, she made mistakes that, when healthy, she would not have made: she forgot things, repeated herself, made writing errors, fell down, had hallucinations, and died an addict's death.

She forgot things sometimes, like a person's name, or her own age, or her pocketbook when she went out (Keckley 368). She repeated herself, perhaps also a kind of forgetting, as when she talked to the clerks on her shopping trips, or when, as a patient at Batavia, she visited Mrs. Patterson and said, "Good morning," over and over again within a few minutes (Batavia records, July 7, August 4).

Early in her life Mary Todd Lincoln wrote careful, insightful, witty letters in a graceful, flowing script. Her later letters, however, were often careless, sometimes incoherent. She made many errors that betrayed her agitated state of mind. In 1868, she referred to Tad as "a very promising lovely boy of 15," and in the same letter referred to his difficult birth 12 years before (Randall 148). In another letter she claimed to have had with Abraham, "every association since I was fifteen years old," even though she had been at least 20 when she first met him (Sandburg 284). In 1869, she made a mistake about the age difference between herself and her husband: "He was 14 years & 10 months older than myself" (Turner 534), when there were in fact only nine years between them. And she forgot how old she was (24) when Robert was born: "I was not twenty, by several months, when my first child was born..." (Turner 536). She referred, in 1874, to her "grandson" Robert Lincoln (Neely 183). She also confused dates sometimes, such as writing 1864 instead of 1873 (Turner 604), and made spelling and punctuation mistakes that she would not ordinarily have made. Similarly, in later years she increasingly lapsed into the lavish use of dashes and commas in place of periods (for example, Turner 546, 552).

Mary Todd Lincoln's elegant handwriting (Goltz, May 29, 1862; Helm 123, Nov 23, 1856) also sometimes became a scrawl, very unlike her normal script. Many an addict has experienced reading, sober, something written in her own hand when she was under the influence of the drug and finding her own handwriting strangely alien and very sloppy. As early as January, 1865, there is a telegram written by Mary Todd Lincoln in a "large, uneven handwriting" (Turner 199). A few months later, before the assassination, she sent Secretary Stanton a message: "In the original manuscript her usually smooth handwriting shows nervousness and agitation" (Randall 375). The Turners describe Mary Todd Lincoln's letters later in that year:

> The letters were filled with garbled instructions and admonitions delivered in the manner of a stern schoolmistress. . . Many of them were scrawled in pencil, some are nearly illegible, others barely coherent. (Turner 248)

Indeed, to avoid just such embarrassing efforts, suffering addicts avoid, whenever possible, writing anything at all. For, as Mary Todd Lincoln wrote in 1870, "my hands tremble so much—I cannot write" (Turner 552). One of the things that often shames an addict is her sometimes shaking hands.

In the insanity file are many examples of Mary Todd Lincoln's normal handwriting and several striking examples of her shaky handwriting. For example, two letters and one fragment which she wrote in the late 1860's (Neely 153, 155, 168) show particular lack of control—writing uneven and severely slanted to the right. Another striking example of her distorted handwriting, also in the insanity file, is something Mary Todd Lincoln scrawled on the back of a livery stable bill (dated Jan. 28, 1874). She used the back of this bill to write an almost illegible, rambling statement that her house should be given to her son after her death. This handwriting almost does not look like hers at all. Then, during the summer of 1878, Mary Todd Lincoln's letters "flowed out in all directions, some of them almost illegible where her script had once been clear and graceful" (Ross 327). And by 1882, "her once exquisite handwriting" had become "as huge and unformed as that of a child" (Turner 707). The contrast between Mary Todd Lincoln's early, normal handwriting and her later, distorted handwriting is shown clearly in the Turners' collection of her letters, page xiv.

Another physical sign of an addict's illness is falling, usually for no apparent reason. The real reason may be impaired coordination or weakness from malnutrition or just plain wooziness. In December, 1879, Mary Todd Lincoln fell in her apartment in Pau, France. Six months later, still in France, she fell on some stairs. And not long after that, on the return voyage to America, she fell again, this time grabbed to safety by Sarah Bernhardt.

Having hallucinations can be another symptom of chemical addiction, particularly when alcohol and chloral combine. Like falling, having hallucinations is an extreme symptom, not like the every-day symptoms of forgetting and distorted handwriting that we mentioned earlier. Mary Todd Lincoln's hallucinations, although much talked about, occurred mainly during a certain period of her life, approximately 1870 to 1875, before she went to Bellevue and while she was taking chloral. She heard ghostly rappings, conversations with invisible people, voices telling her what to do. She saw her dead husband or sons. The city was on fire. Her only living son was terribly ill. Someone was trying to kill her. Such hallucinations, both visual and auditory, are entirely explainable by her use of alcohol and chloral hydrate, both sedative-hypnotic drugs.

The last mistake an addict makes is when she, usually inadvertently, takes too much. The ultimate mistake is death. According to Mary Todd Lincoln's death certificate, she died from "paralysis," which the doctor later clarified as "apoplexy" (Evans 344). Clearly she slipped into a coma and died. There are two important clues, however, that suggest that Mary Todd Lincoln's final coma was drug induced. First, her constricted pupils indicate that she had opiates in her system. Second, the "boils" she suffered from (Evans 343) were quite likely abscesses, infected needle marks from morphine injections. Her coma and death, then, resulted from the suppression of respiration caused by too much morphine.

In summary, then, Mary Todd Lincoln was almost certainly physically sick with chemical addiction. As her illness worsened, she looked unkempt, lost weight, and appeared sedated. She felt much pain, felt much older than she was, had problems sleeping and eating, had persistent cough, chills, infections, eye problems, and problems retaining fluids. In addition, she forgot things, repeated herself, and her handwriting deteriorated; she fell several times, had hallucinations, and died of an overdose of morphine.

What Treatment Would Have Been Available to Her?

The only "treatment" available for Mary Todd Lincoln was an insane asylum. Because the few institutions for inebriates in this country were for inebriate men only, women addicts who were treated at all were treated as lunatics. There were, of course, the poor lunatics who were treated in badly-run, under-staffed places that could provide little more than incarceration. And there were the aristocratic lunatics like Mary Todd Lincoln, who were rich enough to afford a private place and fortunate enough to have a loved one to visit them there and oversee their care. Many of these lunatics, poor and rich alike, were really addicts who couldn't stop consuming the chemicals that made them crazy. Mary Todd Lincoln was not a lunatic, but the only hope for helping her arrest her addiction was sending her to an insane asylum.

At the time Mary Todd Lincoln was in desperate need of treatment, there were four recognized asylums for men inebriates in this country. The first such institution was founded in Boston in 1857; then the one in Binghamton, New York, in 1858; the Washingtonian Home in Chicago in 1863; and the Sanitarium in Philadelphia in 1867. None of these facilities took care of women addicts.

It was not until 1882, the same year Mary Todd Lincoln died, that a home for women addicts, the Martha Washington Home, opened in Chicago. This home, with beds for 16 women, was administered by a committee of men and women (three of the women were MDs), and answered a great need in the community:

> For many years the great need of an institution in or near Chicago, for the alleviation and cure of women addicted to the use of opiates and alcoholic stimulants, has been deeply felt. The number of women that have fallen victims to these habits is undoubtedly much greater than is generally believed. (The Martha 5)

The booklet explaining the philosophy of the Martha Washington Home, later known for many years as the Martha Washington Hospital, goes on to say that the opium habit, "so subtly formed, is now prevailing to an alarming degree among the middle and higher classes of society" (The

Martha 6). The author points out that the victim of intemperance, whether from opiate or alcohol, becomes "nervous," loses all will power, and needs special treatment away from home, but not in an insane asylum:

> Physicians, especially, have often longed for such a retreat as the Martha Washington Home for many patients, who, although they cannot be properly controlled in their homes, yet are not subjects for an insane asylum. (The Martha 6)

Mary Todd Lincoln was not a subject for an insane asylum, but there was, in 1875, no other place to send her.

Unfortunately, the staffs of even the best insane asylums that could provide the most personal care did not understand about addiction. Thus the treatment they provided consisted merely of substituting other mood-changing drugs for the addict's preferred drug. In Mary Todd Lincoln's case, it seems evident from her behavior that she went to Bellevue addicted to laudanum (which she supplemented with other drugs). And while she was there her behavior changed:

> After Mrs. Lincoln's release from Batavia and until her death she behaved differently. A change had come over her and she was quite unlike her former self. She was no longer aggressive or offensive; she fought no battles, indulged in no hysteria. (Evans 309)

Most likely this change in behavior was the result of the medication she received at the asylum. Although her records there are very incomplete and most likely altered, we can infer that she, like so many of the other women there, was given morphine. She would *not* have been given laudanum or chloral hydrate, to which she was already addicted. Robert Lincoln would have made certain that the doctors knew to avoid those drugs. But morphine would have quieted her, would have turned her into the different Mary Todd Lincoln that Dr. Evans described. It would have made her passive as long as she had enough of it. It would have convinced some people, if they wished to be convinced, that she was indeed, by 1876, sane once again (or at least less troublesome).

Mary Todd Lincoln, who had two brothers who were addicts, was genetically vulnerable to chemical addiction. It is evident from her erratic behavior that she too had a destructive relationship with mood-changing chemicals. Because of the pain she suffered and because of her station in life, she had access to alcohol, laudanum, and morphine. Her son Robert arranged for her to have the only treatment that was then available for a woman addict, an insane asylum.

To Sum Up

Mary Todd Lincoln was a very bright and able young woman who loved life and loved her family. A nineteenth-century Barbara Bush. She suffered from headaches, for which the best doctors gave her the best pain medicine: opiates. They gave her laudanum, the standard pain medication, which she probably supplemented with alcohol in the form of brandy, and which she later supplemented with chloral hydrate. Then as morphine, injected by the hypodermic needle, became the most advanced treatment for pain, the doctors most likely gave her that. Vulnerable to chemical addiction, which also afflicted two of her siblings,

Mary Todd Lincoln took the medicine prescribed in good faith by her doctors. She became an opiate addict. Like the classic chemical addict, she suffered a downward spiral of deterioration, both physical and mental, as evidenced in her increasingly erratic behavior. Her son Robert placed her in an insane asylum, but he was unable to keep her there. She died with infected needle marks on her body, a victim of chemical addiction disease.

Her son Robert and her husband Abraham also suffered because of her disease. As we now know, this insidious disease destroys the addict and simultaneously damages the addict's loved ones even as they try to help her. Robert and Abraham were co-dependents, loving family members who increasingly focused on Mary Todd Lincoln's behavior in their earnest efforts to control it.

Robert saw it all. He remembered Springfield life, knew his Todd relatives, was at Harvard when his family moved to Washington, and served in the war on General Grant's staff. When his father was killed, Robert, at age 22, had to interrupt his law studies and move to Chicago, taking responsibility for his young brother (age 12, with educational difficulties) and his distraught mother. Some years later, when his mother's erratic behavior grew worse, he contrived to send her, at great risk to his own reputation, to an insane asylum. A few months later he acquiesced to her removal from this asylum. A few months later still he relinquished control of his mother's financial affairs, giving her once again access to her own money, even though there was still evidence that she was not her normal self.

Why? He obviously did not have the first trial because he wanted her money. He obviously did not really believe her insane (in the usual way) or he would not have allowed her to be released so soon. He must have realized that she was an addict (after all he had her followed by Pinkerton men) and in his desperation decided that a "good" insane asylum was the only possible way for an addicted woman to receive treatment. He was desperate to help her.

And indeed, in the insane asylum, his mother did behave better. She was subdued, no doubt because of the morphine she was surely given, and she gave the staff no trouble. Robert visited her there regularly and kept in touch with the doctor in charge. Robert had been much criticized, however, for putting his mother there, and when concerned people began to try to get her out, Robert finally agreed, reluctantly probably, but he was tired of being the "bad guy."

Whether Robert thought his mother's change in behavior meant that she was cured, we will never know, but most likely he feared the worst, that she would begin to act crazy again. At any rate, she fled to Europe, where he did not hear from her for four years. Stoically, he lived with his mother's fury at him for what he had done to her.

What he had done, however, was *for* her. He had arranged what we might now call an intervention on her behalf. He had arranged for her to be taken off, as lovingly and discreetly as possible, to the best treatment facility that he could locate. His desire was to help her, to save her. And he did all this with the full knowledge that no one, least of all his mother, would appreciate his effort and his pain.

As is still often the case with co-dependent people, who have developed certain skills for coping (at great personal cost, unfortunately) with addicts, Robert Lincoln had other experiences in his life with addicts. In 1867, his first law partner, Charles T. Scammon, was alcoholic and sent to treatment in the East. And Robert's wife Mary was apparently also alcoholic.

Robert's father, Abraham Lincoln, was always sympathetic toward people addicted to alcohol, stating publicly that non-addicted people were no better, just more lucky and more healthy than alcoholic people. Indeed, in his personal life, there had been many painful examples of addiction.

Lincoln's father, Thomas, may well have been alcoholic, for he moved around a lot and ended up with nothing, occasionally needing financial help from his son, who was dutiful, but distant. Thomas Lincoln's uncle, also named Thomas Lincoln, and his wife were both definitely destroyed by alcohol.

Abraham's beloved stepmother, Sarah Bush Johnston Lincoln, taught him to avoid alcohol, and she was proud that he always did. She had been married previously to a Daniel Johnston, who had serious money troubles, finally landed a job as the local jailor, and housed his wife and three young children in the jail building. He died early (possibly from alcohol) and deep in debt; his widow, Sarah, married Abraham's father. Her son, John Johnston, most certainly was alcoholic, and tried many times to wheedle money out of Abraham, who answered him with patient, fatherly advice.

Lincoln's first business partner, William Berry, was alcoholic, and when their store folded, Lincoln was left with debts which took him many years (well into his marriage) to repay. Lincoln's long-time law partner, William Herndon, was alcoholic. In the early years, Lincoln occasionally bailed him out of jail, and even as a busy president, Lincoln always indulged him. (Robert later commented that he could never understand why his father stuck with crazy Herndon all those years.)

We have many examples of the way Abraham protected his wife Mary. He no doubt worried about her, despaired about her addiction. Mariah Vance (p 142) describes Abraham, in desperation, grabbing Mary's bottle of paregoric one day, chopping it with an ax, and burying the pieces in the ground (the familiar pouring-the-vodka-down-the-kitchen-sink attempt to make things better). Another example occurred during Mary's very public outburst shortly before the assassination, when the Lincolns and the Grants and other dignitaries were reviewing the almost-victorious Union troops. Mary screamed and swore and carried on. Witnesses said that Lincoln winced, but gentled her, and later made excuses that she was ill.

At Lincoln's second inauguration, his vice president Andrew Johnson embarrassed him by giving a drunken speech. His general, Ulysses S. Grant, who finally won his war for him was alcoholic. As was John F. Parker, the man (a cousin of Mary Todd Lincoln's) who was supposed to be at the door guarding Lincoln that night in Ford Theater. Parker was in the saloon next door when Lincoln was shot and killed by John Wilkes Booth, also alcoholic.

Abraham Lincoln understood addiction and its victims better than most people did, better than most people do now. And perhaps in more ways than even he realized, he himself was also a victim. His reluctance to name his wife's illness, for example, and his obsessive desire to control the union and keep it, at all costs, intact, could be considered typical co-dependent behaviors. These are examples of two ways in which a bright and sensitive person who loves an addict tries to bring some sense into his world.

Mary Todd Lincoln certainly suffered from her addiction. She may well have had other illness also. But the dominant and disastrous theme of her life was addiction.

Let us remember Mary Todd Lincoln as a brave lady in pain. It cannot be easy to suffer gracefully while a wary nation watches.

"Mary Todd Lincoln," I would say to her now, "you were truly a woman of courage."

"Courage?" she might reply with some astonishment. "It was my husband, wasn't it, who had the courage, not me. I raised the boys, I dressed well, if I do say so myself. I fixed up the White House. I carried on with receptions and dinner parties, even though the enemy was at the gates. I tried to do what was expected of me, but none of that was about courage, surely."

And I would reply, "You left Lexington, Kentucky, to live on the frontier in Illinois. That took courage. You sorted through your suitors and refused to settle for any but the one you wanted, penniless Abraham, in spite of what your wealthy family thought. That took courage. You encouraged him to follow his political ambitions even though doing so left you alone with the children much of the time and with very little money. That took courage. You, one of the best educated women in the country, who had always had slaves to do your daily work, learned how to cook and clean and wash and iron and care for children. That took courage. You went to Washington as a First Lady from the South who opposed slavery. You sat in hospitals, comforting northern soldiers who had been wounded by people you grew up with. That took courage. You befriended a freed slave woman and treated her like an equal in a time when even many people who opposed slavery would hesitate to do so. That took courage. You buried your husband and three of your sons. That took courage. And above all, Mary, above all this even, you struggled with the pain in your head. That certainly took courage."

Mary would look stunned. "But people have always made me sound so difficult," she might say. "So bad."

"Not me," I'd say. "I think you did a good job, frilly dresses and all."

"Why, thank you," she might say, "for overlooking my mistakes."

"We addicts have to stick together," I'd say.

"But I do wonder what Abraham would say about your calling me an addict." Mary would say.

"Well," I'd say, "I'm pretty sure he would just say that you were the prettiest and smartest and cuddliest addict he ever knew."

Appendix: What We Now Know about Chemical Addiction

Addiction is an elephant sitting on your face. With the weight of him there you can't get any air and with the smell of him there you wonder why you want any air, but, increasingly, getting air is all you can think about because you must have air. You must have air, any air, no matter what. Like a drowning man, you have no room inside your tortured brain to think about why you need air or how it will make you feel or how much it will cost or what makes that elephant sit on your face instead of on someone else's. It doesn't matter how kind you are or how smart you are or how rich you are. All that matters is that you get that air. You must get it and you will get it any way you can. Or you will die.

Addiction is sort of insanity. A chemical craziness that kills.

Addiction is a disease that tells you sincerely that you haven't got it, because if there is anything wrong, it's something else that's wrong, maybe with you, but most certainly with the people close to you. It tells you this over and over again while it kills you.

Addiction is something that only certain special people have. It is a soft, green worm burrowed in your brain, sleeping there. Perhaps you don't even know he's there. But if you waken him and nourish him with the chemicals he craves, he will grow huge and fat and crunchy, filling up your head. He will push and bulge and scrape in there until he squeezes you into a dark and scary corner, trapped against the wall of your own head. Huddled there, you hear your own screams, you smell your own vomit and you feel your own warm waste run down your leg. Before you die.

Chemical addiction is all of these things.

Before we define it in a more conventional way, however, it is important to stress one unique quality of chemical addiction. This uniqueness lies in its sheer power. It is this raw and awesome power that renders its victims ever more desperate, crazy, blind, and frightened as it gradually kills them. It sickens the victim's body, twists her personality, deadens her intellect, and paralyzes her spirit. Indeed, the force of addiction is probably the most powerful thing in the realm of human experience. It is this extraordinary power that we must always keep in mind as we discuss addiction and try to understand it.

The power, the urgency of addiction, is all-consuming, literally enslaving. It is this power that fuels any addiction, whether to food or sex or gambling or whatever, but here we are focusing on chemical addiction. We are talking about something like the time you were caught in a crowd in a public place where there was no bathroom available and no bushes either and you had to relieve yourself but couldn't find a place to do it discreetly until relief was all you could think about and the pressure was so terrible that you no longer cared about discretion or about anything else but just that one thing. Multiply this urgency by millions and you perhaps can imagine the force (some call it demonic) that fills an addict's brain and heart and soul.

This power is the single most important thing to know about addiction. Because of this inexorable force, there seems to be one fundamental truth about chemical addiction: chemical addiction is never a part of a person's story. It *becomes* her story, always the *same* story. In other words, no matter who you are in the beginning, the addiction disease gradually blots out your individual traits and twists you into a generic addict, the tragic, deluded central character in your own addict narrative that has the same plot as every other addict's story. Only a few, however, ever live to tell this story.

Everything else we know about addiction is secondary to our awareness of this power. I will now try to summarize what else we know about chemical addiction. Although the problem of addiction is an ancient one, the formal study of it is still in its infancy. Yet already we feel that we know a few basic and useful answers to some of the important questions about addiction:

1. What is chemical addiction?
2. Who is most in danger?
3. What drugs are dangerous to them?
4. How do the victims behave?
5. What treatment is available to them?

What Is Chemical Addiction?

Chemical addiction is a destructive relationship between a person and a mood-changing drug. Like a love affair gone bad.

It is a *destructive* relationship because it maims the addict and her family before it kills her. (Obviously, the addict can be female or male, but I will use pronouns referring to the former.)

It is a *relationship* because at first the person and the drug hit it off very nicely. The drug really helps with something—helps wonderfully. Maybe it helps with her pain or social awkwardness or energy level or some kind of stress. At this point there is no problem of control in the relationship because the person controls the drug—uses it whenever she chooses to use it. The drug is her slave, always ready to do her bidding. Also, she likes the drug, may even think of it as a wonder drug because it is so useful to her. This is the first stage of the relationship.

At this point the person appears to be using her alcohol or marijuana or prescription or whatever in just the same way that others around her are using the drug. Of course, she does not want to become an addict—in fact this thought probably does not even cross her mind. Nor will her family be alarmed. With so many of us using so many mood-changing chemicals all the time, no one will notice this person in the first stage of a relationship with the drug, for she is doing just what many others do, appreciating her drug.

The difference between this person and the people around her is not apparent to others, but the difference is there. For she, unlike the others who merely make use of the chemical, already has a relationship with it. She and the drug don't just spend evenings together, they are already involved. The pre-addict person does not know this, however. She thinks they are just getting acquainted.

In the second stage, which may last days, months, or even years, the drug exerts some control over the person, but neither she nor most people around her probably perceive this control. Indeed, she still feels in full control of the drug, although she probably no longer remembers the original help it gave her. In fact it may not exactly help her anymore. It is just a part of her life. Not an important part, she would be quick to say. She does, however, always remember to take her pills along (even though she may forget her toothbrush), or she does always manage to have her wine before dinner (even though she may forget breakfast). The battle of control is well underway.

Let's stop a minute. It is important to realize here that the addict is not "doing this to herself." She is already on a bio-chemical escalator, but she does not know it. Even if she is able to go without her drug for periods of time, the poison is already working in her brain. Her thinking processes regarding her relationship with her drug are already impaired. As the relationship grows, then, so will the impairment.

By the third and last stage, the balance has shifted completely and the drug is in total control of the person. She no longer merely uses the drug, nor merely needs the drug. She *must have* it. She must have it to live, just as she must have air to breath. At this point it is obvious to those around her that she is caught in the vise of addiction. The drug controls her every thought and action, and *she* has become the slave.

Thus, chemical addiction is a destructive relationship between a person and a mood-changing drug. In more specific words, it is a disease of the metabolism (a gap in the immune system, perhaps). It is a primary disease, which means that it must be dealt with first before the addict's other problems can be addressed. It is a bio-chemical disease, not a behavioral one, which means that the addict's craziness is a result of, not a cause of, her illness.

The addiction disease has certain symptoms, which include the compulsive, progressive use of a harmful chemical and the increasing loss of behavioral control. That is, the addict repeatedly consumes the chemical (to ward off withdrawal), needs more and more of it (as her tolerance builds), will do anything to get it (as her obsession grows), and becomes increasingly unable to control how she will act with the chemical inside her. It is important to note that in defining this disease, it is not necessary to specify which chemical is used, how much is used, or how often. The point is that the drug use results in a negative personality change and a loss of control of behavior. Even if the addict sees the danger she is in, the cells of her body have now changed and she must use that drug to enable them to function "normally." This medicine that her cells now need, of course, is the very poison that will eventually obliterate them: the irony of chemical dependence.

Yes, this disease goes by many names. Chemical addiction, chemical dependence, alcoholism, drug addiction, or just plain addiction. In former days it was called inebriety, habitual drinking, dipsomania, narcomania, among others. For practical purposes, these names are interchangeable.

By whatever name, chemical addiction remains the number one destroyer in our country. If we could make a giant graph on our computer screen with bars stretching out to represent the number of deaths from each heart attack, cancer, automobile accident, murder, suicide, for example, and then ask the computer to subtract from each bar the number that were alcohol-induced, those bars would shrivel drastically. Not to mention a similar graph of victims of rape, armed robbery, assault, child abuse, and hospital stays resulting from falls, from stomach, lung, and kidney troubles.

Although we have no such actual graphs before us, even if we were confronted by such startling evidence, most of us would probably not want to believe it. For the web of chemical addiction touches the lives of so many of us. A conservative estimate is that there are more than 20 million addicts among us. Probably more. (Equivalent to one in every ten people you know.) Since we know that each addict snarls the lives of those closest to her as well, we can add perhaps 80 million more people who are directly affected by addiction. The more we think about it, the more still we could add. Yet the more addiction taints our lives, the harder it is to see. Perhaps it is too close. Perhaps we don't want to see. But it is there in staggering proportions.

In summary, then, chemical addiction is a bio-chemical disease characterized by 1) compulsive use of a harmful, mood-changing drug, 2) inexorable increase in the amount used, 3) a loss of control over behavior, and 4) a negative personality change. These symptoms become increasingly unmanageable as the addict is sucked into the inexorable downward spiral.

Who Is Most in Danger?

Chemical addiction runs in families. Like an invisible slinky, a vulnerability to chemical addiction is passed on in the genes. This is the clear consensus of observation and research.

Yet it is at this point that many people say, "Yes, but. . ." Yes, but some people live under terrible stress and surely this makes them vulnerable to addiction? No. According to what we know today, if we could study 100 fraternity brothers living in the same house, under the same stresses, drinking beer whenever they wanted to, only 10 of them would eventually become addicts. Similarly, if we could study 100 first ladies, each of whom took medicine for bad headaches and lost three children and had her husband murdered and lived through a civil war with loved ones on both sides, not all of them would become addicts. About 10 of them would. Because all that terrible stress would trigger addiction only where there was a vulnerability already present.

The exact location of this vulnerability is still being investigated. Brain research and genetic research will no doubt specify this vulnerability someday. Meanwhile, however, the practical information that we already have is loud and clear: if there is alcoholism or other drug addiction in your family, you are a high risk.

It is as simple and as complicated as that.

It is complicated for at least two reasons. The first complication is that because of the stigma of addiction, the addicts in a family are often camouflaged and not easy to identify. The invalid aunt, the eccentric sister, the uncle who "never amounted to anything," the grandfather nobody ever talks about, the brother who was in prison, the one who was married three times, the one who died young of a heart attack. Any of these people could have been addicts, but if they were addicts, it is unlikely that the rest of the family would have been able to use that difficult word, *addict*. Maybe, "He drank a lot, but he didn't have a problem." Or, "She was sick a lot, and had to have her medicine."

Now not everybody who has mental problems or changes jobs a lot or takes a lot of medicine or even drinks a lot is an addict. But when certain things such as these go wrong, chemical addiction is the first and most logical hypothesis to eliminate. So when you ask yourself if there is addiction in your family, it may really be hard to answer that question. You just may not be able to. Or a generation of teetotalers in your family may obscure the original reason for the teetotalism.

The second thing that complicates the simple information that addiction is inherited is that our culture brainwashes us with the idea that one particular chemical, alcohol, is good. Good in moderation. Good for celebrating, relaxing, having fun. Good for becoming successful, sexy, rich, sophisticated. Good for the heart. Many organizations, including our government, profit financially from this idea of the "goodness" of alcohol. Thus most of us are exposed to this dangerous drug at a young age and never question its place in our lives. It does not occur to us that a drug is only one way, of many ways, to make our brains feel good. And that, for some of us, it is a deadly way.

In this context, then, if you do know that chemical addiction runs in your family, it becomes extremely hard for you to examine your own use of the common chemicals that might very well be dangerous to you. Not to drink alcohol, for example, becomes a difficult decision (because everybody around you does), even though you know that this decision could very well save your life. And save the people you love most from the pain you would inflict upon them.

Who is most in danger? Anybody who uses dangerous drugs (including the legal ones, like alcohol, one of the most dangerous drugs of all) takes some risk. If you use enough of a drug, you can become addicted. But people who have chemical addiction in their families take an enormous risk, like driving down the windy, narrow river road at 95 miles an hour at night. Some of them are most likely very "addictable."

What Drugs Are Dangerous to Them?

The mood-changing drugs, the psychoactive drugs which affect the central nervous system, are the most dangerous to these addictable people.

There exist many charts, some of them quite bewildering, which show the different categories of mood-changing drugs. Basically, however, there are five categories that concern most of us:

1) **Stimulants**, including cocaine, crack, amphetamines, methamphetamine, methylpheridate, Dexedrine, ice, diet pills.

2) **Opioids**, including heroin, morphine, codeine, paregoric, methadone, Suboxone, Dilaudid, Fentanyl, OxyContin, Vicodin, Percocet.

3) **Depressants,** including alcohol, chloral hydrate, barbiturates (such as phenobarbitol), and benzodiazephines (such as Valium, Librium, Klonopin, Xanax).

4) **Cannabinoids**, including marijuana and hashish.

5) **Hallucinogens**, including LSD, mescaline, ecstasy, GHB.

This list is not intended to be exhaustive, only to show the major categories and to mention the most common drugs within them.

There are two important points to be made about this list of categories. One is that the drugs in *all* five categories are dangerous to the addictable person. And the other important point is that once a person becomes addicted to a drug in one category she is immediately addicted to all the other drugs in that category, and extremely vulnerable to the drugs in the other four categories as well. This concept is known as cross addiction, or cross tolerance.

Cross addiction means that your mother who became alcoholic drinking mostly gin, cannot be safe scaling "down" to "only wine." Cross-addiction means that if your father is alcoholic, you should not say to yourself, "I will stay away from alcohol, but anything else is okay," because the valium or the codeine that a doctor might prescribe for you could hurt you just as much as alcohol. Cross addiction means that an addiction to one drug cannot usually be treated by substituting another drug.

In other words, if you are allergic to sugar, you would be fooling yourself to stay away from cakes and pies, but allow yourself all the ice cream you want. Or we could not treat the sugar addict by depriving him of desserts, but providing him with plenty of soda and chewing gum.

Thus, to addictable people, *all* the mood-changing drugs are dangerous. If you are vulnerable to addiction, any one or combination of these drugs can touch the addiction trigger in your brain. Your brain will not care that these drugs have different names. That fat, green worm in there loves morphine just as much as it loves alcohol.

How Do the Victims Behave?

Crazy. If you object to that word, we can say chemically crazy. Active addicts, regardless of who or what they were before they became addicted, regardless of which drug they were first addicted to, act like addicts. Chemical addicts act alike. Or at least enough alike to fit a pattern, an addict profile. These addicts all have the same disease, addiction, and one symptom of this disease is a predictable unpredictability of behavior.

This unpredictability worsens gradually. It only flickers at first, but as addicts become more and more preoccupied with this private battle, they behave more and more like the typical addict and less and less like themselves. This growing unpredictability is often perceived by others, and indeed also by the addict himself, as craziness. It is temporary craziness, however, induced by the chemicals, and it is a result of the addiction, not the cause of it.

Chest pains, for example, are often a symptom of heart attack. Often, but not always. But because of the critical nature of a heart attack, chest pains are always alarming, and usually checked out in the hope that a heart attack hypothesis can be eliminated. Similarly, there are certain warning signs of addiction. Any one of these signs, like chest pains, is not enough for a diagnosis, but a cluster of these signs points dramatically to addiction.

Active addicts, regardless of which drug they are first addicted to, act *increasingly*, but not consistently: afraid, angry, withdrawn, desperate, and physically sick. Remembering that each of these five adjectives describes a category of typical addict behavior, but that not every addict will behave in all these ways all the time, let us examine each category.

Active chemical addicts are increasingly ***afraid***. Many of their fears are vague, so they appears nervous, sometimes, jittery. Later on they may become suspicious, paranoid, even hysterical. They may be afraid of a big thing, like being abandoned, or they may pinpoint their fears and become fearful of particular things, such as heights (bridges, for example) or loud noises (like telephones). The point is that they, quite rightly, sense danger and they grow more and more nervous because they cannot be sure where the danger comes from. A key word here is *nervous*.

Active chemical addicts are increasingly ***angry***. Unexpectedly moody, touchy, irritable. They become resentful, often blaming others for their problems. They have sudden outbursts of unreasonable anger, and then later are contrite, apologetic, genuinely remorseful because they feel guilty about the outburst. A key word is *touchy*.

Active chemical addicts are increasingly ***withdrawn***. Because of their preoccupation with the battle, their obsession with their drug, they grow more and more self-centered, secretive. They trust other people less, care about them less, and become lonely, selfish, and sorry for themselves. They are hard to talk to, hard to reach, and they neglect their friends. They also neglect their own values, doing more and more things that they formerly would have considered immoral. As their hopelessness deepens, they act more and more upset. A key word is *depressed*.

Active chemical addicts are increasingly ***desperate***. They try ever more desperately to control their lives: to change job or house or spouse or even to change from one drug to another. Because money is one of the easiest things for them to control, they may have bursts of extravagance or of miserliness. They may shop or gamble or telephone excessively. And throughout all this, they will be denying things (another attempt at control): denying that anything is wrong at first, and then denying that they need any help fixing it, and then at last denying that it can be fixed at all. A key word is *controlling*.

Active chemical addicts are increasingly unwell, ***physically sick***. Eventually, as the addiction worsens, their body shows the wear and tear. There will be marked deterioration in their weight, complexion, appearance, appetite, and sleeping patterns, for example. They may sometimes appear lethargic, sedated, dazed. They may be prone to infections that they seem unable to throw off. They may appear forgetful, sometimes confused, and unable to concentrate. They may even have hallucinations—see and hear bizarre things. Their coordination also suffers, as noticed in their handwriting, their tendency to have accidents that involve falling. In addition to this general physical deterioration, they will also have certain physical difficulties associated with specific drugs, such as gum and stomach problems from alcohol, bowel and eye problems from opiates. A key word is *deteriorating*.

In summary, then, the victims of addiction, the chemical addicts, behave in certain ways. Their behavior becomes increasingly unpredictable and erratic—baffling to the people who know them best. They act more and more, in ever-increasing spurts, afraid (nervous), angry (touchy), withdrawn (depressed), desperate (controlling), and physically sick (deteriorating). These are the behavioral symptoms of the classic addict.

What Treatment Is Available to Them?

Not so long ago, it was assumed that all addicts faced a dire fate—jail, insanity, or death. There was almost never a way out.

Today, however, terrible as it still is, chemical addiction can sometimes be treated. Although some drugs are thought to be more addictive than others (like heroin), and some are known to be more toxic than others (like alcohol), treatment now focuses more on the person than the drug. The person must take responsibility (and stop blaming other things and people) for his own life and learn how to live again. No easy task, to be sure.

Treatment begins with time to let the chemicals wash out of the person's system (detoxification). Then addicts must learn to understand and accept their disease and to live without mood-changing chemicals (abstinence). They must gradually pick up the shattered pieces of their original selves and begin gluing them back together. They must teach themselves to be honest and grateful. They must make amends and curtail resentments. In other words, they must strive to be more rigorously humble and forgiving than sometimes seems humanly possible.

This healing process takes time. After all, you don't fall off a 600-foot cliff and then just get up and go home and cook supper.

Today, most successful treatment of chemical addiction, whether in-patient or out-patient, includes the principles (12 steps) of Alcoholics Anonymous or Narcotics Anonymous. We don't know why they work, but we are grateful that some people make them work sometimes. Hence, the word *infancy* for our understanding of addiction treatment.

To sum up, then, chemical addiction is a destructive relationship between a person and a drug. In this relationship the drug physically, spiritually, and emotionally enslaves the person who must repeatedly use the drug even though it distorts him or her.

The people most vulnerable to addiction disease (the ones most likely to be addictable) are the people who have chemical addiction in their families.

To these addictable people, *all* the mood-changing drugs are highly dangerous.

Addicted people unwittingly behave increasingly like the classic addict: predictably unpredictable, chemically crazy. They act afraid, angry, withdrawn, desperate, and physically sick.

Even though our understanding of chemical addiction is still primitive, we know that addiction victims can be treated. Successful treatment usually includes abstinence within the spirit of a 12-step program.

Let us remember that many amongst us are still, right now, suffering as Mary Todd Lincoln did. With the proliferation of prescription drugs that affect the central nervous system, with the still pervasive hesitance among physicians, dentists, and psychiatrists concerning addiction, and with the probably 30 million especially addictable people in our country, the climate remains much the same as it was when Mary Todd Lincoln sought relief from her debilitating headaches. Today many people are terminally ill with chemical addiction and even more are in grave danger.

Today, however, women addicts do not need to go to insane asylums where they are given different, but equally dangerous, drugs. Today, for a Mary Todd Lincoln, there is hope.

Bibliography

"Abuse of Chloral Hydrate": *Quarterly Journal of Inebriety*, (January, 1880): 53-54.

Alcoholics Anonymous. New York: Alcoholics Anonymous World Services, 1976.

"An Extraordinary Case of Opium Inebriety." *Medical Record* 12 (1877): 239-40.

Badeau, Adam. *Chicago Tribune*. January 17, 1887, p. 10.

Baker, Jean H. *Mary Todd Lincoln*. New York: Norton, 1987.

Beard, George M. *Stimulants and Narcotics; Medically, Philosophically, and Morally Considered*. New York: G. P. Putnam, 1871.

Beasley, Joseph D. *Wrong Diagnosis, Wrong Treatment*. Durant, Oklahoma: Creative Informatics, 1987.

Bellevue patient progress reports, photographic slide copies, Louis A. Warren Lincoln Library and Museum, Fort Wayne, Indiana.

Berger, Philip A. and Keith H. Brodie, editors. *Biological Psychiatry*, Volume 8 of *American Handbook of Psychiatry*. New York: Basic Books, 1986.

Berry, Stephen. *House of Abraham*. New York: Houghton Mifflin, 2007.

Boyden, Anna L. *War Reminiscences or Echoes from Hospital and White House*. Boston: D. Lothrop, 1887.

Bradford, Gamaliel. Wives. New York: Harper, 1925.

Breecher, Edward M. *Licit and Illicit Drugs*. Boston: Little, Brown, and Co., 1972.

Calkins, Alonzo. *Opium and the Opium-Appetite.* Philadelphia: J. B. Lippincott, 1871.

———. "Opium and Its Victims." *Galaxy* 4 (1867): 25-36.

Carpenter, William B. *On the Use and Abuse of Alcoholic Liquors in Health and Disease.* Philadelphia: Blanchard and Lea, 1855.

Chicago Inter Ocean 20 May 1875.

Chicago Inter Ocean 21 May 1875.

Chicago Times 20 May 1875.

Clinton, Catherine. *Mrs. Lincoln.* New York: Harper Collins, 2009.

Cobbe, William Rosser. *Doctor Judas.* Chicago: S. C. Griggs, 1895.

Cole, H. G. *Confessions of an American Opium Eater.* Boston: James H. Earle, 1895.

"Confessions of a Young Lady Laudanum-Drinker." *Journal of Mental Science* 34 (1899): 545-50.

Courtwright, David T. *Addicts Who Survived.* Knoxville: University of Tennessee Press, 1989.

———. *Dark Paradise.* Cambridge: Harvard University Press, 1982.

Crothers, T. D. *Morphinism and Narcomanias from Other Drugs.* Philadelphia: W. B. Saunders, 1902.

Day, Horace B. *The Opium Habit.* New York: Harper & Brothers, 1868.

Dennett, Tyler. *Lincoln and the Civil War in the Diaries and Letters of John Hay.* New York: Dodd and Mead, 1939.

DeQuincey, Thomas. *The Confessions of an English Opium-Eater.* London: J. M. Dent, 1930.

Detzer, Eric. *Odyssey of an Opium Eater.* San Francisco: Mercury House, 1988.

Dipsomania, Dr. D'Unger's Cure for Drunkenness. Chicago: 1879.

Emerson, Jason. *The Madness of Mary Lincoln.* Carbondale: Southern Illinois University Press, 2007.

Epstein, Daniel Mark. *The Lincolns.* New York: Random House, 2005.

Evans, W. A. *Mrs. Abraham Lincoln: A Study of Her Personality and Her Influence on Lincoln.* New York: Knopf, 1932.

Friedman, Jane M. *America's First Woman Lawyer.* Buffalo: Prometheus Books, 1993.

Frisch, John R. "Our Years in Hell: American Addicts Tell Their Story, 1829-1914." *Journal of Psychedelic Drugs* 9 (1977): 199-207.

"General Facts About the Use of Opium in This Country." *Quarterly Journal of Inebriety* 2 (1878): 214-17.

Goff, John S. *Robert Todd Lincoln.* Manchester, Vermont: Friends of Hildene, Inc., 1969.

Goltz, Carlos W. *Incidents in the Life of Mary Todd Lincoln.* Sioux City, Iowa: Deitch and Lamar, 1928.

Grob, Gerald N., ed. *Nineteenth-Century Medical Attitudes Toward Alcoholic Addiction.* New York: Arno Press, 1981.

Hambly, Barbara. *The Emancipator's Wife.* New York: Random House, 2005.

Hay, John. *Lincoln and the Civil War in the Diaries and Letters of John Hay.* New York: Dodd, Mead & Co., 1939.

Helm, Katherine. *The True Story of Mary, Wife of Lincoln.* New York: Harper, 1928.

Hirschhorn, Norbert. "Mary Lincoln's 'Suicide Attempt': A Physician Reconsiders the Evidence." *Lincoln Herald*, (Fall, 2003): 94-98.

Hirschhorn, Norbert and Robert G. Feldman. "Mary Lincoln's Final Illness: A Medical and Historical

Reappraisal." *Journal of the History of Medicine and Allied Sciences* (1999): 511-42.

Hickey, James T. "The Lincoln Account at the Corneau & Diller Drug Store, 1849-1861." *Journal of the Illinois State Historical Society* 77 (1984): 60-66.

Hubbard, Fred H. *The Opium Habit and Alcoholism*. New York: A. S. Barne, 1881.

"Hypodermic Use of Opium." *The Probe* 1 (1869): 7-9.

Insanity File. Louis A. Warren Lincoln Library, Fort Wayne, Indiana.

Johnson, Vernon E. *I'll Quit Tomorrow*. New York: Harper & Row, 1980.

Kane, H. H. *Drugs That Enslave*. Philadelphia: Blakiston, 1881.

Keckley, Elizabeth. *Behind the Scenes*. Salem, New Hampshire: Ayer, 1868.

Keeley, Leslie E. *The Morphine Eater*. Chicago: Palmer & Co., 1881.

Ketcham, Katherine, and Ginny Lyford Gustafson. *Living on the Edge*. New York: Bantam, 1989.

———, and L. Ann Mueller. *Eating Right to Live Sober*. Seattle: Madonna, 1983.

Kinnaird, Virginia. "Mrs. Lincoln as a White House Hostess." *Papers in Illinois History*. Springfield: Illinois State Historical Society, 1939.

Latimer, Dean, and Jeff Goldberg. *Flowers in the Blood*. New York: Franklin Watts, 1981.

Layard, J. C. "Morphine." *Atlantic Monthly* 33 (1874): 697-712.

Levine, Harry G. "The Discovery of Addiction." *Journal of Studies on Alcohol* 39 (1978): 143-74.

Levinstein, Edward. *Morbid Craving for Morphia*. London: Smith, Elder, & Co., 1878.

Lindesmith, Alfred R. *Addiction and Opiates*. Chicago: Aldine, 1968.

Ludmerer, Kenneth M. *Learning to Heal*. New York: Basic Books, Inc., 1985.

The Martha Washington Department of the Washingtonian Home of Chicago, Illinois. Chicago: James & Morse, 1882.

Maxwell, Ruth. *Beyond the Booze Battle*. New York: Ballentine, 1986.

———. *The Booze Battle*. New York: Ballentine, 1976.

M. D., "The Personal Experience of an Ex-opium Habitue." *Medical Record* 13 (1878): 399-400.

Milham, James R. and Katherine Ketcham. *Under the Influence*. New York: Bantam, 1983.

Miner, N. W. Letter in *Chicago Tribune* 21 April 1888: 15.

Morgan, H. Wayne. *Drugs in America*. Syracuse: Syracuse University Press, 1981.

———. *Yesterday's Addicts*. Norman: University of Oklahoma Press, 1974.

Morgan, Roberta. *The Emotional Pharmacy*. Los Angeles: The Body Press, 1988.

Morris, F. Baldwin. *The Panorama of a Life*. Philadelphia: George W. Ward, 1878.

"Mrs. Lincoln's Obsessions." *Illinois Magazine* 23 (1984): 20-22.

Mueller, Ann and Katherine Ketcham. *Recovery*. New York: Bantam, 1987.

Musto, David F. *The American Disease*. New York: Oxford University Press, 1987.

Neely, Mark E. and R. Gerald McMurtry. *The Insanity File*. Carbondale, Illinois: Southern Illinois University Press, 1986.

"Nervous Headaches Cured by the Inoculation of Morphia." *Southern Medical and Surgical Journal* 1 (1838): 514.

Nicolay, John G. and John Hay, Ed. *Complete Works of Abraham Lincoln*. New York: Lincoln Memorial University, 1894.

O'Brien, Robert and Morris Chafetz, editors. *The Encyclopedia of Alcoholism*. New York: Facts of File Publications, 1982.

Ohlms, David L. *The Disease Concept of Alcoholism*. Belleville, Illinois: Gary Whiteaker Company, 1983.

O'Neill, Eugene. *Long Day's Journey Into Night*. New Haven: Yale University Press, 1955.

O'Neill, John and Pat. *Help to Get Help*. Austin, Texas: Creative Assistance Press, 1989.

"Opium-eating." *Lippincott's Magazine* 1 (1868): 404-09.

Ostendorf, Lloyd, and Walter Oleksy, editors. *Lincoln's Unknown Private Life*. Mamaroneck, New York: Hastings House, 1995.

Packard, Elizabeth. *The Prisoner's Hidden Life*. Chicago: 1868.

Parssinen, Terry M. *Secret Passions, Secret Remedies*. Philadelphia: Institute for the Study of Human Issues, 1983.

Petersdorf, Robert G., ed. *Harrison's Principles of Internal Medicine*. New York: McGraw-Hill, 1983.

Pusey, William Allen. *A Doctor of the 1870's and 80's*. Baltimore: Charles C. Thomas, 1932.

Randall, Ruth Painter. *Mary Lincoln: Biography of a Marriage*. Boston: Little, Brown, 1953.

Rhodes, James A., and Dean Jauchius. *The Trial of Mary Todd Lincoln*. Indianapolis: Bobbs-Merrill, 1959.

Roe, Daphne A. *Alcohol and the Diet*. Westport, Conn.: AVI Publishing, 1979.

Ross, Ishbel. *The President's Wife, Mary Todd Lincoln*. New York: B. P. Putnam, 1973.

Ross, Rodney A. "Mary Todd Lincoln, Patient at Bellevue Place, Batavia." *Journal of the Illinois State Historical Society* (1970): 5-33.

Royce, James E. *Alcohol Problems and Alcoholism*. New York: The Free Press, 1981.

Rush, Benjamin. *Effects of Ardent Spirits upon the Human Body and Mind*. Brookfield: E. Merriam & Co., 1814.

Sandburg, Carl. *Mary Lincoln, Wife and Widow*. New York: Harcourt and Brace, 1932.

Schreiner, Samuel A., Jr. *The Trials of Mrs. Lincoln*. New York: Donald I. Fine, 1987.

Schwartz, Thomas F. "My Stay on Earth is Growing Very Short." *Journal of the Illinois Historical Society* (Spring, 1970): 5-33.

Seymour, Richard B., and David E. Smith. *Drugfree*. New York: Sarah Lazin, 1987.

Stables, Gordon. "The Confessions of an English Chloral-Eater." *Belgravia* 26 (1875): 179-90.

Stoddard, William O. *Inside the White House in War Times*. New York: Charles L. Webster, 1890.

Suarez, John M. "Mary Todd Lincoln: A Case History." *American Journal of Psychiatry* (Jan., 1966): 816-19.

Swett, Leonard. "Letter to David Davis, May 24, 1875." *Davis Family Papers*, Illinois State Historical Library, Springfield.

Terry, Charles E., and Mildred Pellens. *The Opium Problem*. New York: Committee on Drug Addictions, 1928.

Townsend, William H. *Lincoln and His Wife's Home Town*. Indianapolis: Bobbs-Merrill, 1929.

Turner, Justin G. and Linda L. *Mary Lincoln—Her Life and Letters*. New York: Knopf, 1972.

Van der Heuvel, Gerry. *Crowns of Thorns and Glory*. New York: Dutton, 1988.

Weil, Andrew, and Winifred Rosen. *Chocolate to Morphine*. Boston: Houghton Mifflin, 1983.

"What Shall They Do To Be Saved?" *Harper's Magazine* 35 (August, 1867): 377-87.

Williams, Roger J. *The Prevention of Alcoholism Through Nutrition*. New York: Bantam, 1981.

Made in the USA